C000295301

Commendations for
What's wrong with human rights

Rarely have I read such an informative, historically accurate, and biblically correct book. David Cross has clearly defined why the matter of *'human rights'* is one of the most serious issues of the day. This book is an in-depth *"Divine litmus test"* that is desperately needed in a world of increasing entitlement, lawlessness and humanly defined, so-called inalienable rights, which contrast sharply with the values and rights constituted by a Sovereign God.

In these pages, David offers profound hope in a failing society – a society that is trying to re-define itself morally, ethically, politically and even re-define God! But, in the end there will be grave consequences, as Isaiah reminds us – *"Woe to those who call evil good and good evil, who put darkness for light and light for darkness, who put bitter for sweet and sweet for bitter"* (Isaiah 5:20).

Not only do I enthusiastically endorse this book, but it is my fervent hope that it finds its way into the hands of every serious seeker of truth – especially every church and government leader, in as many circles as possible. Be prepared to be challenged and have your Bible close at hand!

Rev. Dr. Alistair P. Petrie
Author – Executive Director
Partnership Ministries
www.partnershipministries.org

This insightful book makes it clear where the human rights movement has gone wrong and deserves serious consideration and analysis. From both a theological and legal perspective, David Cross's juxtaposition of Biblical teaching and misplaced human rights theory is powerful and persuasive. From the Enlightenment onwards, he shows a convincing knowledge of history and philosophy, crafting a dynamic apologetic as to how today's 'rights' movement is in essence a Tower of Babel movement.

What's Wrong with Human Rights is accessible and impressive. David manages to distil extremely complex concepts and philosophical traditions into an understandable and gratifying format which can be enjoyed by anyone whatever their background, from the layman to the graduate student.

By exposing the cracks in today's radical embrace of a rights culture and suggesting a Biblical remedy as the only way back, he has transformed old-school Christianity into the new-school legal world. It is a must read for anyone interested in today's culture wars.

Andrea Minichiello Williams
*Chief Executive for Christian Concern
and Christian Legal Centre*

What's Wrong with Human Rights?

What's Wrong with Human Rights?

Uncovering a False Religion

David Cross

Sovereign World

Published by Sovereign World Ltd
Ellel Grange, Ellel Ministries, Bay Horse, Lancaster, LA2 0HN
www.sovereignworld.com

ISBN: 978-1–85240-873-2

Unless otherwise stated, all Scripture quotations are taken from the New American Standard Bible®, Scripture quotations taken from the New American Standard Bible® (NASB), Copyright © 1960, 1962, 1963, 1968, 1971, 1972, 1973, 1975, 1977, 1995 by The Lockman Foundation Used by permission. www. Lockman.org

Other Bible versions used are:
NIV – NEW INTERNATIONAL VERSION®. Copyright © 1973, 1978, 1984 by Biblica, Inc. All rights reserved worldwide. Used by permission.
NIrV – NEW INTERNATIONAL READER'S VERSION®. Copyright © 1996, 1998 Biblica.
NEW INTERNATIONAL VERSION® and NIV®; NEW INTERNATIONAL READER'S VERSION® and NIrV® are registered trademarks of Biblica, Inc. Use of either trademark for the offering of goods or services requires the prior written consent of Biblica US, Inc.
KJV – From The Authorized (King James) Version. Rights in the Authorized Version are vested in the Crown. GNT – Good News Translation in Today's English Version – Second Edition Copyright © 1992 by American Bible Society. Used by Permission.
The Amplified® Bible (AMPC), Copyright © 1954, 1958, 1962, 1964, 1965, 1987 by The Lockman Foundation Used by permission. www.Lockman.

Cover design by Esther Kotecha, EK Designs
Typeset by Avocet Typeset, Somerton, Somerset, TA11 6RT
Printed in the United Kingdom by Bell and Bain Ltd, Glasgow

I dedicate this book to my wife Denise, with whom I have walked the Christian pathway for nearly forty years. She has encouraged me, challenged me and cared for me in countless ways. I am forever grateful for the enthusiasm she has for life, for family, for adventure and for seeking God's truth. Jesus saved us both individually and as a couple, and the walk with Him has been more exciting and fulfilling than we could ever have imagined.

Contents

Foreword

Peter Horrobin

This is an important book. Why? Because it tackles one of the greatest unrecognised problems of our age – the conflict between what the world understands by human rights and what the God who created humanity says in His book – the Bible.

For many hundreds of years the foundational principles underlying the governance of most of our western nations have been the laws of God and Christian teaching, which together have positively influenced every sector of society. But, since the years of the French Revolution and the constitutional statements in the Declaration of Independence in the USA, a 'new religion' has been slowly gathering momentum. It has rolled down the hills of time in the nineteenth and twentieth centuries to become one of the most powerful influencers of the twenty-first.

This 'new religion' has gathered pace at an alarming rate and has become the clarion call of every pressure group that has been raised up to state a case to society. But while increasing popularity may have lent the doctrine of human rights international credibility, popularity does not trump truth!

I recently visited the Basilica that overlooks the city of Boulogne in France. In this magnificent cathedral is an amazing time-line history map of the world. In the section which covers the French Revolution in 1789, it simply states that this heralded the declaration of the rights of men and citizens, as if man had suddenly discovered something unknown to history and, seemingly, more important than God himself!

I will leave it to David Cross to unpack the history and to colour in the details, but what he has written is not only of real importance and significance for the church but for the whole of society. For, in the camouflage of something which seems so good, a poisonous deception has been creeping in which has no foundation in Scripture. Under the guise of doing what is right for mankind, truth has been subtly moved aside by the juggernaut of human rights ideology.

In this truly ground-breaking book, David has done an amazing job of shining the light of truth from God's Word onto a problem which has previously hardly been recognised. These are days when the Church not only needs to understand what is happening in the world around us, but to recognise when the ground seems to be shifting beneath our feet and get back again on to solid ground.

For those who carry an intercessory burden for the nations, this book is a must-read. Indeed, it should be a must-read for all Christian leaders as they seek to lead God's people through the moral and intellectual maze of twenty-first century ideology. When I first read the manuscript I was gripped by the importance of what David is saying. I pray it will be a blessing to you also.

Peter Horrobin
Founder and International Director
Ellel Ministries International

Introduction – Why this Book?

The intention of these pages is to show that the ideology of universal and innate human rights is not in agreement with the truths given to us in the Bible. As such, it is a concept which, although endorsed by very well-meaning people, will never bring the justice intended by the relentless promotion it is given today. The pursuance of human rights can be a useful tool in giving a voice to those truly oppressed in this world, but it will not give them a solution.

A justice system that prioritises the claiming of rights rather than the acknowledgement of wrongdoing is much more likely to create conflict than to settle it. This is because the definition of those rights is based on a moving pendulum of public opinion. In contrast, God's plumb line of right and wrong is unchanging and so provides an absolute basis for true justice.

The foundational, sometimes called inalienable, rights discussed in this book are not primarily concerned with the various legal entitlements necessarily agreed between a government and its citizens, but the rights which have historically and progressively been assumed to belong to everyone, simply by virtue of their being born human.

I maintain that the Bible is absolutely clear in affirming that every human being has inalienable value, but it contains no inference that God has given any rights to humankind except those that come through a covenant relationship with Him. According to the Bible, that personal covenant relationship is now established only through believing in, and following, Jesus Christ.

The governments of the world are, of course, free to choose

the concept of human rights in their search for international justice, even if, as I believe, it will never bring the expected results. My greater concern is for the Body of Christ. I believe that the increasingly pervasive ideology of innate personal rights is not only harmful to society as a whole but is corrupting the teaching of the Bible, not least in regard to the understanding of sin.

The philosopher Sir Roger Scruton spoke in September 2017 on the BBC radio programme *A Point of View*. He included these significant words:

> *European society is rapidly jettisoning its Christian heritage and has found nothing to put in the place of it save the religion of human rights.*

I couldn't agree more. A *religion* can be defined as a system of beliefs or a rule of life, held with ardour and faith. The increasingly fervent belief in the philosophy of human rights as the answer to the distress which is so evident in this world is indeed best described as a man-made religion, and therefore a false religion. The warning of Paul to the Christians in Colossae seems particularly pertinent.

> *See to it that no one takes you captive through hollow and deceptive philosophy, which depends on human tradition and the elemental spiritual forces of this world rather than on Christ. Colossians 2:8 (NIV)*

I want to make two clear statements. I believe that the ideology of universal human rights offers the world a false hope of true justice, and I also believe that the aggressive promotion of this ideology is removing traditional and necessary boundaries in many areas of human activity, not least in regard to issues of sexuality and marriage. It is my hope that the contents of this book will adequately back up these statements and will also give direction to the only true pathway for rights, justice and wellbeing for humankind: following Jesus Christ.

Chapter 1

Humans have God-given Rights: True or False?

The danger of self-evidence

In 1776, Thomas Jefferson wrote these now famous words in the Preamble to the United States Declaration of Independence:

> *We hold these truths to be self-evident, that all men are created equal, that they are endowed by their Creator with certain inalienable rights...*

This powerful statement has provided a foundation to the American constitution to this day, but is it true? According to Thomas Jefferson, and those who co-signed this historic document, the rights supposedly conferred by God on *every* human being are life, liberty and the pursuit of happiness. It is interesting to note that this claimed truth is described as self-evident rather than being evidenced by the Word of God, for the fact is that nowhere in the Bible is there any indication that He has conferred inalienable rights on human beings, except through the terms of a specific covenant relationship with Him.

Actually, for any true right to be legitimate, it must be conferred by someone with greater authority, able to give that particular entitlement to others. For example, the driving licence issued by the government of any nation permits the holder of that license to drive on the road network of that country, subject to certain conditions. It would be illegal to print your own driving licence and to self-proclaim an entitlement or right to drive on the roads.

I suggest that, in the much more serious matter that we are considering here, such self-proclamation is exactly what much of the world has done with regard to human rights. When viewed from a biblical perspective, humanity's claim to universal and innate human rights is illegitimate. We shall see, as we explore the history of human rights, that this man-made ideology has become a place of faith for governments seeking a means of justice in the world. In the void left by the progressive abandonment of its Christian heritage, Europe in particular has embraced, and exported around the world, a religion of human rights, a religion that is now being spread by aggressive international enforcement.

The growing belief in universal entitlement

Good governance of a nation will always include the giving of specific rights to its citizens, in numerous areas of life such as through the driving licence referred to above. These legal entitlements are established and agreed as a form of contract between the rulers of a nation and those ruled. They have clear boundaries and are written into the laws of the nation. Interestingly, the apostle Paul took full advantage of his right of Roman citizenship to demand an audience with Caesar (Acts 25:10–12).

However, such citizens' rights are not the main issue of

this book. Here we are exploring the historical growth of a philosophy, and now a widespread belief, that every man, woman and child has certain rights, often referred to as inalienable, dependent only on their existence as human beings. The belief has been so strongly promoted that the claiming of entitlement now appears to dominate the ethics of society; it is an age where the declaring of man's rights is replacing any true acknowledgement of man's wrongdoing.

The ubiquitous claiming of rights seems to have become increasingly aggressive and infinitely extendable in scope:

I have a right to personal freedom
I have right to end my life when I choose
I have a right to family and private life
I have reproductive rights, including a right to abort an unborn baby, at any time
I have a right to choose my gender
I have a right to express any sexual identity or attraction in any way I choose
I have a right to healthcare, which includes abortion
I have a right to marry anybody, even myself
I have a right to parenthood, whatever my marital status
I have a right to adopt children, whatever my marital status

It is becoming accepted that, if people do not respect these declared rights, they are to be regarded as bigoted and narrow-minded. But none of these so-called fundamental rights come from the legitimate conferral of a higher authority. There is no inalienable right to parenthood, there is no inalienable right to marriage, there is no inalienable right to even life itself. Each is ultimately a gift from God and comes with clear boundaries and responsibilities.

Children's rights, women's rights, body rights, gay rights, workers' rights, transgender rights, consumer rights, marriage rights, voting rights...the list is endless in today's culture of entitlement, because there is no external code of morality on which the concept of rights is based. There is only a man-made and moveable morality which can add or remove specific rights on the list of those considered inalienable in order to reflect current opinion.

In Geneva, in November 2017, the United Nations Human Rights Committee drafted its most recent official interpretation of the *right to life*. There was a significant focus on the unconditional right of women to have an abortion, while the committee chose to deny any right to life for an unborn child. The illogical nature of today's coercive promotion of human rights was highlighted, in an extraordinary way, by one representative of the committee who commented, "Legal abortion is at the heart of the issue of the right to life."

Questioning the validity of any of these rights in another person's life is immediately classified as discrimination against not just their life-style, but against the person themselves. There seems to be less and less space for sensible debate on the true nature of these rights. Equality, inclusivity and liberty have become like mantras of a new religion of rights, however ill-defined or meaningless these concepts are, in the absence of any supporting moral framework.

I thought that I had heard every extreme of the rights argument until talking to an Anglican vicar recently. He had been in discussion with an atheist who was a particularly ardent sceptic in regard to Christianity. This man had forcefully declared that he definitely didn't need God to tell him how to run his life, which was quite moral enough, as far as he was concerned. And then, as the discussion was coming to a close, he added, "However, if there is a God and if there is a heaven, on the basis of my good life I shall be claiming my right of entry." And he wasn't joking!

What exactly is a right?

The word *right*, as it is being used here, means a conferred authority or privilege in a particular area of activity. It is a just claim of entitlement or a licence to act in a certain way. The word *entitlement* clearly implies something that must be given rather than assumed, and this is a very important issue in understanding the legitimacy of human rights.

If I go fishing on a Scottish salmon river, I will need to obtain permission, a right to fish, given by the relevant owner of the river bank. The landowner is the one with the authority to allow such a privilege. In fact, in giving permission, he delegates something of his authority in favour of the fisherman, within stated boundaries of time, location and methods of fishing. The important point here is that rights can only be truly legitimate if they are conferred by someone with the necessary higher authority. A poacher may decide that he has a right to take fish without the permission of the landowner, because of long-held local views on what is considered acceptable practice. However, poaching remains a self-proclaimed and illegitimate right, likely to be carried out, literally, more in the dark than in the light.

Jesus was able to exert legitimate authority, a right to say and do the things He did, only because that authority had been conferred on Him by the protocol of the Godhead.

> *And Jesus came up and spoke to them, saying, "All authority has been given to Me in heaven and on earth." Matthew 28:18*

A pilot on an aeroplane has the right, the delegated authority, to fly the plane over a designated route according to strict rules of airline protocol. The passengers are comfortable that this right exists by virtue of the higher authority of the airline company, together with the aviation rules that give boundaries to the pilot's delegated authority. That authority is symbolised by the uniform that every airline pilot wears, giving confidence to the passengers that he or she has a legitimate right to fly the plane. However, if a hijacker stands up on the aeroplane, threatening harm to passengers with a gun unless the flight is rerouted to his requirement, it would be clear to everyone that this self-proclaimed right to redirect the plane is illegitimate and a serious crime. The control of the plane has been gained by wrongful force rather than through rightful authority.

I shall be saying in this book that the humanist ideology of universal and inalienable rights is the equivalent of a hijack of the true human rights given by God and conferred through a covenant with Him (John 1:12). This hijacking of human rights is just as real as when a terrorist over-rides the true authority given to an aeroplane pilot.

Increasingly these days, countless human rights are assumed to be innate privileges to which we are entitled simply by virtue of our human existence. Many governments have decided that these innate natural rights need to be enshrined in law so as to become the legal rights of each individual, by which each nation seeks to establish a just society, and to help regulate international behaviour. If such inherent rights do exist, by whom have they been conferred? Remembering the examples of the fisherman, the poacher, the pilot and the hijacker, what higher authority has declared that, from our birth, certain fundamental rights exist for every man and woman? Christians, seeking to walk in biblical truth, need to ask a very important question: "Are universal rights, without righteousness, truly legitimate?"

Followers of Jesus are in the world but not of it
How much has this ideology of rights been adopted within the church? The pastor and writer David Wilkerson said many years ago, "The church used to confess its sin, now it confesses its right." Is that true? What does the Bible say about rights or entitlements? What does God say about true justice according to His Kingdom values? As followers of Jesus, how do we answer

those who say that rights such as those listed on previous pages are entirely reasonable and fair? In this book, I shall seek to uphold the teaching of Jesus rather than surrendering to the pressure of human opinion.

The insistent demands of rights-based justice challenge the very core of the teaching of Jesus, not least in the area of forgiveness, for example. The more the world says that we should stand firm on all our personal rights, the more difficult it can be for a follower of Jesus to give up a seemingly fundamental and very reasonable right of recompense from those who have hurt them. Jesus says that the only way for each of us to know true peace is to forgive unconditionally, and yet this is often regarded as weakness by those advocating the importance of victims' rights. The Bible encourages us to take active care that we are not deceived by the philosophies of the world, however well-intentioned (Colossians 2:8). We will discover, I believe, that the concept of claiming foundational human rights, outside of a covenant relationship with God, is indeed a deceptive philosophy and not the ultimate answer for creating a just society.

A number of Christian commentators, at odds with the current liberal tendencies of the Church of England, have suggested that the leadership of the Church has, in many of its current Synod discussions, re-defined justice as the pursuit of the rights of the victim rather than the pursuit of what is objectively right. If true, this is a dangerous slide into agreement with modern humanism and disagreement with the Word of God. The influence of the world upon the values of the Kingdom of God should always be very carefully discerned. We are called to be salt and light in this spiritually bland and dark world (Matthew 5:13), but that saltiness is lost if the Body of Christ blindly adopts the wisdom of man rather than the wisdom of God. Truly we are *in* this world, to have a life-giving impact, but we should not be *of* the ways of this world (John 17:16).

Problems with rights

Here is just a tiny selection of the thousands of newspaper headlines that have appeared over the last few years relating to the challenging, conflicting, and often very confusing issues of human rights:

Doctor MPs Stand Against 'Right to Die'.

"What about My Family Rights?" Says Father of Girl Killed by Asylum Seeker.

Six in Ten Crooks Use Human Rights to Stay in Britain.

UN Busybody Compares Britain's Eviction of Travellers to Human Rights Abuses in Zimbabwe.

Refugee, Convicted of Sexually Assaulting a Child and Slashing the Face of an Adult with a Broken Mirror, is to Receive Substantial Damages for His Unlawful Immigration Detention...to Vindicate His Rights.

At Last, Equality Police Decide Christians Do Have Right to Follow Beliefs.

Child Rapists Taken off Sex Offenders' Registry in Secret. Police Say It's to Protect their Human Rights.

Professor with Down's Syndrome Son Says, "I Support Eugenic Abortion, it Helps Disability Rights."

Right-Wing Extremist, Responsible for the Deaths of 77 People in Norway in 2012, Claims that the Norwegian Government has Violated the European Convention on Human Rights by Holding Him in a Maximum-Security Prison.

Hillary Clinton blasts Trump: "Abortion is a Human Right."

"Killing Unborn Children is Not a Human Right," Says USA State Department.

Former Irish President Claims that Baptism Violates a Baby's Human Rights

UK House Speaker, John Bercow: LGBT Human Rights must trump Religious Liberty

The law courts are constantly experiencing difficult decisions in seeking to balance competing arguments in pursuance of individual human rights. Many of these rights are declared as wholly valid irrespective of personal bad behaviour, what the Bible calls sin. Even in secular society many people today are troubled by the frequent conflicts between supposed rights and clear responsibilities. Some years ago, a man was imprisoned in England after he raped and strangled his niece. At the European Court of Human Rights he claimed, and was given, a right to vote in all United Kingdom parliamentary elections. The Supreme Court of the UK has since disputed that judgment, as convicts in the UK have never before had that privilege, and this issue has remained unresolved for more than a decade.

Recently a demonstrator, standing outside a courthouse that was considering a case about rights, carried a banner saying, "Don't make a moral wrong a human right." Why does it seem that so often human rights legislation conflicts with our sense of what is morally correct? Could the answer be simply that the whole concept of universal human rights is not God's idea?

The inevitable conflict of rights

A contract of legal entitlements and duties between a government and the citizens of a nation makes very good sense. However, to imply that there are certain human rights for every person, which are inalienable (something from which we cannot be separated), is not only biblically unsafe but will inevitably lead to the problem of competing rights. Trying to define and balance the opposing claims of people's so-called rights turns out to be little short of a nightmare.

Is my right to freedom, however that is defined, more important than your right to freedom? For example, in Northern Ireland each year we hear arguments by one faction of the society saying, "I should surely have the right to express my religious or political beliefs by marching with bands and chanting through your neighbourhood." "But surely," says the other faction, "I should have the right to enjoy peace and quiet in my neighbourhood, without the intimidating sound of your views being expressed so strongly." According to Jesus, the answer to this conflict is not for each side to shout their rights louder but rather for both sides to love God and to love their neighbour better. How wonderfully simple!

> "'Love the Lord your God with all your heart, with all your soul, with all your mind, and with all your strength'. The second most important commandment is this: 'Love your neighbour as you love yourself'. There is no other commandment more important than these two." Mark 12:30–31 (GNT)

Another rights conflict that has created much heated argument over the last few years is the right claimed by same-sex married couples to adopt a child. Some adoption agencies have been forced to close down, and some individuals have been dismissed from serving in adoption courts, because they have expressed the view that the right of every child to grow up under the traditional parenting of a mother and father should take precedence over the desires and rights of a gay couple. God's laws do not lead to such a dispute over competing rights but simply require our willingness to abide by His clear instructions for our lives, not least in the area of marriage and family.

From the evidence of centuries of human conflict, very often over disputed entitlements of every kind, God's way of defining what is right and what is wrong, providing a framework of justice for the human race, is both sensible and workable. Why change it?

Are human rights universally accepted?

In 1948, chaired by Eleanor Roosevelt, and following the devastation of World War II, a group of well-intentioned philosophers, religious leaders and intellectuals from around the world proposed a new template for international justice. This group, speaking, in effect, on behalf of the human race, concluded that a new charter, The Universal Declaration of Human Rights, should define the pathway for future international justice. Whilst some Christians, such as Jacques Maritain, played an important role in drafting the declaration, the plan was to avoid any specific religious input likely to divide opinion. Instead, they sought a consensus of what some described at the time as practical morality. Although well-meaning, such a consensus necessarily obscured widely differing views concerning human nature, not least the Christian belief in the concept of sin. The decision to exclude religious precepts, however understandable, surely energised the spirit that lies behind the modern secular humanism so dominant today.

There was no suggestion as to what authority was being invoked to declare such rights as, once again, they were seen as natural or self-evident from man's perspective. In trying to find a historical justification for this strategic political declaration, reference was made to documents such as the Magna Carta in England and the Cyrus Cylinder from Persia. Interestingly, this second ancient text relates to the Jewish people being granted freedom of movement and worship during the Babylonian exile. This text was actually far from being a declaration of foundational human rights, but rather a statement of reasonable governance and restraint by those ruling.

Despite the secular nature of the 1948 declaration, the underlying moral code was largely based on Judeo-Christian

Western values, and a number of nations regarded the rights listed as inappropriate for their own cultures. Sharia Law, for example, would be inherently opposed to the concept of human rights, because Muslims say that the will of Allah needs to be the arbiter of justice, rather than following a man-made philosophy of human entitlement.

To say that notions of goodness, equality, liberty and rights are universal, transcending state borders, is simply wishful thinking, as religious ideologies, national culture and self-interest will invariably result in competing views of entitlement for each nation, much less for individuals. The concept of human rights may indeed have given a voice to the oppressed, but has this been at the expense of targeting the true problem of sinful behaviour by both individuals and governments?

So what really is wrong with the idea of human rights?

The quick answer is, "A great deal!" This book is arguing that the concept of universal innate human rights is fundamentally flawed as the basis for a code of justice, because it is simply not God's idea. In many countries where laws have historically been based on Judeo-Christian principles, the intrusion of a rights-based system of justice has, I believe, brought huge confusion and very little, if any, improvement in the moral climate. Interestingly, Dwight D Eisenhower, a former American president, said at his first inaugural address in 1953, "A people that values its privileges above its principles soon loses both."

However, the primary purpose of these pages is not to embark on a political argument for or against human rights but to suggest that, for followers of Jesus, this way of pursuing human wellbeing is not consistent with the culture of the Kingdom of God. We cannot necessarily persuade the world of its mistaken adoption of this concept, but we can avoid defiling the Body of Christ with the intrusion of a belief in entitlements that is simply not true. Once again, let's be very clear: the Bible certainly tells us that we each have innate value, but because of humankind's sinful rebellion against God, we have no innate rights.

The world finds sin to be an embarrassing concept, a moral perspective which is regarded by many as completely outdated in this apparently post-Christian age. Basing a system of justice on biblical precepts of sin has become uncomfortable for modern society, so the world now increasingly promotes justice through the declaration of human rights in order to avoid the need to address, or more importantly confess, the real issue of human wrongs.

The foundational search for what is right

God has put within humankind a deep desire for justice. That includes a belief in the need for security, significance, belonging and freedom, all provided when we know, without doubt, that we are children of God. Without this deep spiritual security in God's provision of justice we search for man-made alternatives. An innate sense of justice is one of the things that separates us from animals. It is unlikely that the most intelligent of animals ever says to itself "That's not fair," but throughout the Bible we see man's search and contention with his Maker regarding what is right. Job was certainly not happy with the way he believed God had treated him.

> *Don't condemn me, God. Tell me! What is the charge against me? Is it right for you to be so cruel? To despise what you yourself have made? And then to smile on the schemes of wicked people? Job 10:2–3 (GNT)*

By the last chapter of the book of Job, he has realised that God's wisdom is far beyond his own and he accepts that God must surely know what is truly just.

I know, LORD, that you are all-powerful; that you can do everything you want. You ask how I dare question your wisdom when I am so very ignorant. I talked about things I did not understand, about marvels too great for me to know.
Job 42:2–3 (GNT)

Sadly, the world, for the most part, has not come to the same conclusion as Job. The rejection of God's wisdom and justice has inevitably left a void in our feeling of security which philosophers, leaders and politicians have tried to fill through the centuries. In this void the man-made ideology of rights has become established, but sadly, it will never answer the human heart-cry for true freedom and security, aspirations which can only be met by being reconciled with God.

While walking on this earth, Jesus radically challenged his disciples' view of justice. He announced the startling news that, in His Kingdom, it is right to love your enemies, it is right to turn the other cheek when slapped by an opponent, and it is particularly good to surrender our right to be recompensed by those who have hurt us, in favour of forgiveness. Jesus told many parables that would have shocked His followers, turning upside down their strongly held beliefs about fairness. In Matthew chapter 20, He tells of a vineyard owner who paid the same wage to each labourer, irrespective of the hours worked, making it clear that in His Kingdom, God will always treat each person in the way that He knows is equitable. He truly does have the inalienable right to deal with His creation as He chooses, however much that might challenge our own sense of justice.

"They took their money and started grumbling against the employer... 'Listen, friend,' the owner answered one of them, 'I have not cheated you. After all, you agreed to do a day's work for one silver coin. Now take your pay and go home. I want to

*give this man who was hired last as much as I gave you. **Don't
I have the right to do as I wish with my own money?** Or are
you jealous because I am generous?'" Matthew 20:11–15 (GNT,
bold added)*

There has always been a difference between what sinful man
thinks is right and what God says is right, but we live in days
where, in many nations, divine and human definitions of justice
are diverging very rapidly. Once the unchanging plumb line of
God's truth is abandoned in favour of the moving pendulum of
secular humanism, there is no limit to what society can decide
is right. Just a few years ago it would have seemed inconceivable
to most people in Britain that the definition of *marriage* could
be changed by an arbitrary vote of Parliament, after millennia
of unquestioned clarity. But, by ignoring the wisdom of the
Bible and basing moral arguments simply on the need to meet
people's stated rights, such redefinitions become inevitable.
Sadly, the door is now open to any meaning for marriage that
fits current fashion.

The defining of rightness and justice in UK society seems
now to depend far more on the strength of activist groups than
on the customary and common laws, based on Judeo-Christian
principles, which have served the nation so very well for many
hundreds of years.

The spiritual significance of human rights

The reference in the United States Declaration of Independence
of 1776 to the Creator of human life being the originator of
universal human rights reflected an understandable desire, at
the time, for divine endorsement of a new ideology of rights.
Sadly, it was an endorsement that was in fact just wishful
thinking. The concept of innate human rights is entirely man-
made, perfectly plausible as a way of ordering society. However,
because it is biblically unsound, it must surely give considerable

opportunity to the spiritual ruler of the world, Satan, to cause havoc with human justice.

We shall be looking later in this book at a significant point in history when France, during its bloody revolution of 1789, made a momentous declaration of the Rights of Man. This strategic document was deemed to have been overseen by a spiritual entity referred to in the preamble as the *Supreme Being*. This deity is clearly not the God whom Christians worship, but is boldly proclaimed as the one having ultimate spiritual authority over this historical declaration. We have here a glimpse into the spiritual reality behind two contending systems of justice, one driven by a philosophy of man's rights (promoted by a false god) and the other driven by the need to deal with man's sin (revealed by the God of the Bible).

God has only conferred rights on His creation within a covenant relationship with Himself, an offer, incidentally, which the majority of the world has so far rejected. We shall later consider more specifically the enemy's strategies through the promotion of universal human rights. Suffice it to say here that, if Satan can successfully steer mankind away from a belief in the need to deal with sin, the only one that ends up with an increase in legitimate spiritual rights is Satan himself!

For advocates of rights:
which ones do we actually have?

Philosophers during the period of history known as the Enlightenment found this question, of what should be on the list of natural rights, an even harder task than formulating the basic concept of rights itself. We will look later at some of their writings in a little more detail, but John Locke, for example, proposed that the foundational entitlements for every human being should be the right to life, liberty and ownership of property. He also added to these the ultimate right of revolution by the populace where a government failed to respect the assumed basic rights.

We should note that a right to armed rebellion against a government will be found nowhere in the teaching of Jesus. Even at the time of John Locke's writings, some immediately questioned the validity of these stated rights, which not only ignored divine conferral, but were, they argued, self-centred and an unhelpful encouragement to public disorder.

A right to life, liberty and the pursuit of happiness, a right to equality, a right to security of property, a right to employment, a right to family life, a right to privacy, a right to defend life and liberty, all these and many more have found their way into numerous constitutions and declarations that have sought to define a just society based on the idea of natural human rights. This difficulty in establishing an unchanging list, and in finding an adequate definition for each of these apparent rights, points to a flawed basis for the whole philosophy.

The word *natural* has been adopted by theorists and politicians through the centuries to imply the self-evident and foundational nature of particular rights. The right to life, for example, seems so obvious that it has been concluded that it must be reasonable to assume such a right exists. Let's take a moment to look at this right to life. On the face of it, there seems to be every reason to assume that this must surely be an innate right of humankind. But consider the situation of someone attacking your life. Many people would say that there must inevitably be occasions when life-threatening behaviour by someone invalidates their own right to life; we must, in an extreme scenario, kill or be killed, but who decides when this so-called fundamental right of our opponent is to be taken away?

There's always going to be a problem in deciding when one person's right to life outweighs that of another person. In fact, we shall continue to see that this conundrum of competing rights is one of the fundamental flaws of any system of justice based on claiming innate entitlements. I have mentioned that, despite pleas from more than one hundred governments and pro-life organisations, the United Nations Human Rights Committee, meeting in Geneva, made a decision to exclude unborn children from the right to life in international law. The right of a mother to take the life of her unborn child has been prioritised over the right of the child to continue living. This is a clear example of both the uncertain morality of rights ideology and the inevitability of competing interests.

The CEO of an American organisation promoting abortion was recently asked, "In your opinion, at what point does an unborn child get constitutional rights?" The CEO answered, "Well, I don't know really, I don't know that there's an exact answer for that. It's not the point."

But it is the point! The Bible approaches the value of human life from a completely different angle. God has given clear instructions regarding our behaviour towards one another, not least in the foundational command, "You shall not murder." He also makes it clear that, because of sin, our natural entitlement is rather to death than to life.

> *The LORD says, "Now, let's settle the matter. You are stained red with sin, but I will wash you as clean as snow. Although your stains are deep red, you will be as white as wool. If you will only obey me, you will eat the good things the land produces. But if you defy me, you are doomed to die. I, the LORD, have spoken." Isaiah 1:18–10 (GNT)*

> *For sin pays its wage – death; but God's free gift is eternal life in union with Christ Jesus our Lord. Romans 6:23 (GNT)*

Sin clearly has a consequence, which can affect the wellbeing of each one of us, both spiritually and indeed physically. Claiming a God-given basic right to a trouble-free life, irrespective of our sinful behaviour, is contrary to the teaching of Jesus. He considered it very important to warn the man whom He healed of paralysis at the pool of Bethesda.

Afterward, Jesus found him in the Temple and said, "Listen, you are well now; so stop sinning or something worse may happen to you." John 5:14 (GNT)

The definitive list of apparently self-evident rights turns out to be less obvious than we are led to believe, particularly if we consider the truths of the Bible. We'll look at the validity of some of the other basic rights in due course. Many have argued that the so-called inalienable rights of man are always going to be in irresolvable conflict with responsibility. Natural rights have got mixed up with natural ability and natural value, which are truly innate and inalienable, and are consistent with the Word of God. The concept of sin promotes human responsibility, while the concept of natural rights seems often to promote human selfishness.

In summary

A right is an entitlement conferred on a person by another who has the authority to give such entitlement. In order for foundational and innate human rights to be legitimate, they must be conferred as part of our creation. Some have argued that God has indeed given universal basic rights simply as a part of our human existence, but this cannot be supported by the Bible. Some have argued that such rights are a self-evident aspect of human development, which must be enforced by law, in order to bring justice in the world. However, the Bible says that it is only the resolution of man's sin that brings true justice, not the claiming of man's rights. Furthermore, Jesus expressly teaches us to forgive rather than to claim a right of retribution against those who have hurt us.

Self-evidence is surely a very unsafe foundation for such a far-reaching ideology as the existence of universal human rights. For a follower of Jesus Christ, God has made clear in His Word that humankind has inalienable value but not inalienable rights, except within a covenant relationship with God.

Chapter 2

A Little Early British History About Claiming Rights

The birth of customary and common law

It may be helpful to consider how the language of rights began to be used in Britain. Before the arrival of Christianity, the statutes of law were passed on orally. King Alfred codified a Book of Laws (893AD) that blended the ancient oral customs and previous written Saxon codes with significant biblical precepts. Alfred especially focussed on mercy, and he also gave particular importance to a passage from Matthew:

Therefore all things whatsoever ye would that men should do to you, do ye even so to them: for this is the law and the prophets. Matthew 7:12 (KJV)

Or as King Alfred chose to write it:

What ye will that other men shall not do to you, that do ye not to other men.

These words were intended to form a basis for justice between neighbours, as well as between a judge and a plaintiff. The laws, as they developed, were not so much imposed by those ruling as developed through use and custom among the people. There was no mention here of innate rights but rather a sense of foundational Christian duties that were of benefit of the whole community.

There was an understanding that God's laws, as defined in the Bible, were not only a way of finding true relationship with Him, but they also gave a code of law that would bring justice and wellbeing to the community if they chose to walk by His statutes. When, for example, God says, "Do not commit adultery", He is defining behaviour which will give order to society through marriage and family. There is no hint in the Bible that such order will come through each person standing on his or her God-given rights. Jesus Himself was not averse to respecting human law, such as the paying of tax due to Roman authorities, but He also knew that it was only meeting divine law, which He had come to fulfil, that would truly solve the plight of man (Matthew 22:15–21).

After the Norman invasion of 1066, a national common law became established in Britain, particularly through the wise counsel of King Henry II. He divided the country into four parts and appointed judges to execute justice among the people, also introducing juries into a new role of deciding cases, continuing a sense of customary rather than imposed law. Unfortunately, for all his significant improvements in the structures of justice in the nation, he perpetuated one grave error: he still held that the king was above the law, divinely appointed and therefore, to all intent and purposes, infallible. Sadly, his son King John was only too keen to continue the assumption of this supposed *divine right*.

King John needed to be put in his place

On meadows adjacent to the River Thames at Runnymede, to the west of London, in 1215, King John signed a very significant document, the Magna Carta or Great Charter. Interestingly, this document started with these words:

> *...Before God, for the health of our soul and those of our ancestors and heirs, to the honour of God, the exultation of the holy church, and the better ordering of our kingdom...*

Unfortunately, nine weeks after signing, King John reneged on his written promises to the barons who had drawn up the charter, and he arranged for it to be overturned by the Pope, although a form of the document continued through his son Henry III. This charter and subsequent amended versions have been seen by many historians as the start of a formal recognition in England of the importance and validity of human rights, expressed by sentences such as this:

> *No freeman can be imprisoned except by the law of the land and the judgement of peers...*

However, we need to be careful with this assessment. The reason that the barons, the powerful aristocracy of the day, were pressing the king to sign this document was not to promote an idea of English people having certain God-given rights. It was, in fact, written in order to demand that the king should no longer consider himself able to act above the law of the land. King John had been particularly harsh towards his subjects and very exacting towards the barons in requiring them to provide money for his military ambitions. Quite frankly, they had had enough!

What we do see here is a document that sowed important seeds for an understanding that there needed to be some form of contract between those governing a nation and those being governed. This contract of entitlements and boundaries of authority would later be called, by some Enlightenment writers, a *social contract*. Though not a human rights document as such, we must not belittle the significance of the Magna Carta, which has been recognised as a strategic document in many parts of the world, in reminding national leaders that they should never assume that their position entitles them to rule with an absolute authority, in defiance of a just legal system protecting every citizen. It has become an important part, at least symbolically, of modern constitutional government in Britain.

Time for the king to start sharing government with the barons

Drafted in 1258, by a group of barons led by Simon de Montfort, the Provisions of Oxford forced King Henry III of England to accept a new way of governance. Once again, this document was not so much detailing rights for the people as providing a practical means of limiting the authority of the king. This document is regarded by many as England's first form of written constitution following the Magna Carta.

The power to decide the form of government was placed in

the hands of a council of twenty-four members, twelve selected by the crown, twelve by the barons. This council selected men to supervise ministerial appointments, local government and the custody of royal castles. Parliament, which was to meet three times a year, would monitor the performance of this council.

The Scots wanted freedom from the English

In 1320, the Declaration of Arbroath, often described as an historic and strategic plea for man's right to liberty, has been seen by some commentators to be of equal importance to the Magna Carta in initiating modern democracy. The author of this Scottish declaration, assumed to have been the Abbot of Arbroath, actually wrote the declaration in the form of a letter to the Pope asking for his intervention in the quarrel between the Scots and the English.

In fact, the Declaration of Arbroath has very strong parallels with the United States Declaration of Independence some 450 years later, when there was a very similar desire to challenge and remove the rule of an English king.

Significantly, the letter declares that the will of the people should be above that of the king. The choice of monarch should be by merit rather than by supposed divine ordinance, and he should be able to be removed if found to be betraying the people.

In Scotland, at this time, Robert the Bruce was the one to whom the people chose to owe allegiance rather than to the English monarch. However, probably the most significant aspect of the document was the passionate desire of the signatories to be free of English rule, resulting in an oft-quoted passage claiming in effect the right of the Scots people to secure this freedom even at the risk of death:

> *...for, as long as but a hundred of us remain alive, never will we on any conditions be brought under English rule. It is in truth not for glory, nor riches, nor honours that we are fighting, but for freedom – for that alone, which no honest man gives up but with life itself.*

Stirring words indeed, but our battle for freedom, from God's point of view, is not against people, whether fellow citizens or rulers, but against the accusations, temptations and spiritual authority of the enemy.

> *Put on all the armour that God gives you, so that you will be able to stand up against the Devil's evil tricks. For we are not fighting against human beings but against the wicked spiritual forces in the heavenly world, the rulers, authorities, and cosmic powers of this dark age. Ephesians 6:11–12 (GNT)*

The values of God's Kingdom are very different from the values of this world.

More trouble with a difficult king

By the reign of Charles I (1625–1649), who firmly embraced his father's (James I) concept of the *divine right of kings* under the guise of the *royal prerogative*, the absolute authority being exercised by the monarch had once again become an issue of contention. The king was determined to tax the people, using a system of enforced loans to the crown, to pay for his unpopular foreign policies, despite the objections of Parliament. The Petition of Right, in 1628, written by Parliament, is perhaps one of England's most significant constitutional documents. In words reminiscent of the Magna Carta, it contained four main points to curtail the absolutism of the monarch:

- No taxes to be levied without Parliament's consent.
- No English subject to be imprisoned without cause, thus reinforcing the right of habeas corpus.
- No quartering of soldiers in citizens' homes.
- No martial law to be used in peacetime.

The document finishes with these words:

> *All which they [the Members of Parliament on behalf of the people] most humbly pray of your most excellent Majesty as **their rights and liberties, according to the laws and statutes of this realm**... [and they] shall serve you according to the laws and statutes of this realm, as they tender the honour of your Majesty, and the prosperity of this kingdom.*

So here we have another attempt to produce a working social contract between the monarch and parliament (representing the people), advocating reasonable restrictions and rights for both the monarch and the citizens, in accordance with the law of the land. However, Charles I was not at all amenable to giving up his divine rights, and it did not end well for him, as the civil war between the king and parliament cost Charles his head.

Even more trouble with a difficult king

By 1685, James II had become king of England. Many parliamentarians with influence and military power in Britain had major problems with James: he certainly believed in his absolute and divine right to rule, and furthermore, he was Catholic. James wanted more tolerance towards Catholics and Catholic worship, and the ability to install them into political positions. As a consequence, an invitation was made to William of Orange and his wife Mary (James' protestant elder daughter) by opponents of James, to come to England from the Netherlands and forcibly take the throne, with the military help of English supporters.

The resulting overthrow of James, who escaped to the continent, is known by historians as the Glorious Revolution of 1688, and was, in effect, a bloodless coup, although rather more violent in Ireland. Those who invited William were determined that the newly established monarchy would be strongly bound to the law and to a protestant succession. In 1689, with considerable haste (even resulting in ink blots on the document), they drew up the Bill of Rights, a list of prohibited actions by the monarchy. The king was required to promise that:

- He would not interfere with the law of the land,
- He would not tax without the approval of government,
- He could be petitioned without fear of retribution,
- He would not put in place a standing army without the approval of Parliament,
- He would not interfere with the rightful holding of arms for self-defence,
- He would not interfere with the election of members of parliament.

Added to these requirements the document stated that there would be no excessive bail or cruel and unusual punishments, no church courts and, finally, that parliament would be free to debate without disturbance. This document permanently changed the distribution of authority between the monarch and the people of Great Britain, and led to use of the phrase *constitutional monarchy*: royal authority existing more in name than reality.

There was a parallel document drawn up in Scotland that same year called the Claim of Right. Interestingly, exactly three hundred years later, in 1989, the same title was used for a document signed by many influential people in Scotland in pursuit of government devolution to a Scottish assembly.

What exactly is meant by the divine right of kings?

Throughout the Middle Ages, in Christian Europe, certain passages from the Bible were particularly important in promoting the belief that monarchs should be absolute rulers and answerable to no-one but God. Some people believed the Bible stated that kings should, in effect, be above the constraint of the law of the land.

> *Everyone must obey state authorities, because no authority exists without God's permission, and the existing authorities have been put there by God. Whoever opposes the existing authority opposes what God has ordered; and anyone who does so will bring judgment on himself. Romans 13:1–2 (GNT)*

> *Submit yourselves for the Lord's sake to every human institution, whether to a king as the one in authority, or to governors as sent by him for the punishment of evildoers and the praise of those who do right. 1 Peter 2:13*

Despite the important constitutional milestones of the Magna Carta and subsequent petitions and agreements, the absolutist beliefs of kings in Britain were a frequent issue of contention. Citing these passages from the Bible, English monarchs such as James I, Charles I and James II passionately believed that their position as king was not only established by God but that this divine delegation of authority to rule, a *divine right*, entitled the king to make decisions without reference or submission to anyone else, simply before God alone. In fact, they, and many of their subjects, believed that no-one should have any right of resistance to the king's commands. However, many others, including some Christian writers such as Desiderius Erasmus, had said that the monarch should indeed model divine authority but that this was no excuse for tyrannical behaviour.

James I (who was also James VI of Scotland) was the one who sponsored the production of the famous Authorised English Bible of 1611, partly in an attempt to clarify, through the words used in translation, the importance of church hierarchy. The king was shown to be firmly at the head of that authority structure, accountable to God alone. James' opinions on his divine right strongly opposed the authority of the Pope, a factor contributing to the famous Gunpowder Plot, when a group of Catholic radicals planned to blow up the king and the Houses of Parliament.

As the century progressed, the concept of the divine right of kings was increasingly challenged, and Enlightenment writers such as John Locke fiercely spoke out against such absolute authority being held by a king. As we have seen, by the time of the so-called Glorious Revolution of 1688, the monarch's position had been changed forever in Britain.

Although the governmental authority of the monarch in Britain has been largely surrendered to Parliament, the United Kingdom remains one of the few nations that has retained the ceremony of anointing a new king or queen, to symbolise a setting apart of the head of state by the will of God, and an imparting of spiritual authority. This may not be recognised as particularly relevant by most people in the United Kingdom, but there is surely much consequence in the spiritual health of the nation, depending on the godliness or otherwise of the reigning monarch. Many have been very grateful to God for the faithfulness and integrity of Queen Elizabeth II, who has been the longest serving monarch in British history.

What are we to make of the Bible's instructions about rulers?

Any monarch, like any human being, has a carnal nature. Therefore it is a sure recipe for disaster to conclude that the Bible implies a king should be above the law and answerable to no-one else. The poet and statesman John Milton, writing in the middle of the 17th century, was very forceful in his opinion that kings could just as easily be agents of Satan as agents of God in their manner of rule.

It's certainly true that the Bible says that all authority structures existing in this world have originated from God, even those structures with rulers that have been hostile to the ways of God's Kingdom.

> *Jesus answered [to Pilate], "You have authority over me only because it was given to you by God. So the man who handed me over to you is guilty of a worse sin." John 19:11 (GNT)*

Whilst never condoning sin, followers of Jesus are encouraged to respect the institutions of authority; to pray for, and indeed pay tribute to, those who rule. It's better to seek the salvation of kings than their beheading! The structures of governmental authority in this world are intended by God as a means of wellbeing for humankind. However, those occupying positions of authority are frequently driven more by their carnality than by their godliness, and they, like all of us, must therefore be held to account for their sinful deeds. God longs to see an end to every form of oppression, both physical and spiritual, but it is the sin of all humankind that God wants to expose and cleanse, rather than encouraging a right of the people to insurrection against those in authority.

"The kind of fasting I want is this: Remove the chains of oppression and the yoke of injustice, and let the oppressed go free." Isaiah 58:6 (GNT)

Masters, behave in the same way toward your slaves and stop using threats. Remember that you and your slaves belong to the same Master in heaven, who judges everyone by the same standard. Ephesians 6:9 (GNT)

Sadly, there has been a growing disrespect, in recent times, for leaders in many nations. The rights and will of the people are seen as paramount, and leaders are often ridiculed for holding personal positions of principle which do not follow the popular trend. Of course, to challenge the sinful behaviour of all those in authority is important, but the more we undermine and ridicule them, the more, it seems, they become ridiculous. The Bible does not advocate aggressive satirical comment, unkind exposure of faults or relentless disrespect of those in government, but rather we should earnestly bring them before the Lord in prayer. How different our national wellbeing would be if we truly followed such Kingdom principles.

First of all, then, I urge that petitions, prayers, requests, and thanksgivings be offered to God for all people; for kings and all others who are in authority, that we may live a quiet and peaceful life with all reverence toward God and with proper conduct. 1 Timothy 2:1-2 (GNT)

In summary

The language of people's rights has clearly grown out of a genuine need to respond to oppressive rule. Demands that the citizens of a nation should be able to enjoy various freedoms and rights have always received particular impetus at times of corrupt or tyrannical rule by monarchs or, sadly, by church hierarchy. Although the quest for these freedoms has now developed into a much wider ideology of human rights, legislation during the Middle Ages was concerned much more with curtailing the authority of the king than with the declaring of certain universal rights of humankind.

From the Magna Carta to the Period of the Enlightenment, in Britain at least, it was a determination to systematically transfer legislative authority and power from the monarch to parliament that was foremost in the minds of those pursuing these constitutional changes. The notion of the divine right of kings was increasingly recognised as simply a royal entitlement to a selfish and despotic lifestyle, very far from the intention of the Bible.

We will now look at the period of the so-called Enlightenment when the concept of rights began to change significantly from a useful tool in the pursuit of constitutional order to a philosophy concerning the very nature of what it means to be human. In fact, this next period of history saw the birth of what I am suggesting has become the religion of human rights.

Chapter 3

The Age of Enlightenment and Reason: Reasoning with God or without Him?

An unexpected revelation

Some years ago, I was part of a Christian group visiting the Chateau de Vizille near Grenoble in France. In 1788 this building was the location of a significant assembly of dignitaries that made radical demands upon the king, a step which helped to precipitate the French Revolution. Today the chateau is a museum dedicated to the memory of the Revolution, and contains numerous paintings and exhibits from that time.

Quite unexpectedly, a number of the group who were visiting

with me that day discerned such spiritual darkness in the chateau that they felt uncomfortable about going inside. It was a significant day for me, when I saw the articles of the Rights of Man presented on stone tablets on a wall in the chateau, and I realised for the first time that these rights, declared to be under the auspices of a deity named as the *Supreme Being*, were in direct conflict with the biblical commandments of God. It seemed clear to both myself and those with me that this place, with its many exhibits proclaiming a philosophy in contradiction to the Word of God, was indeed giving spiritual ground to the ruler of this world, as Jesus calls Satan, however innocent were the intentions of those who had set up the museum. No wonder it felt so dark. I had stumbled on an issue that was to give me much to think about over the following few years.

A new philosophy of rights

During the 17th and 18th centuries, a time referred to as the Age of Reason or the Period of the Enlightenment in Europe, radical new ways of thinking were being developed. Spurred on by revolutionary ideas and the spread of printing presses, it was believed that everything could and should be questioned and, if necessary, changed or improved through man's intellect and reasoning. Progress, it has been said, was the opium of the Enlightenment.

Men like Isaac Newton were making extraordinary scientific discoveries, bringing huge benefit to mankind; interestingly, he strongly believed that his findings came from the Holy Spirit and that understanding scripture was more important than pursuing science. However, in the general area of philosophy and religion, the concepts of the Bible were no longer being accepted without question. Rather, it was believed that intellectuals were ready to formulate their own philosophies for life, perhaps in association with Christianity, but unfettered by restrictive Church dogma.

Whereas the issue of rights over the previous centuries had been primarily concerned with curtailing the absolutist ambitions of monarchs, there began to be explored new ideas of law, justice and natural rights, conceived through the intellect of human beings rather than just the writings of the Bible. Over many centuries the supposed divine right of rulers had clearly proven itself to be a very unsatisfactory recipe for the wellbeing of those ruled.

Could it be, philosophers and writers argued, that within each human being there were foundational and universal precepts of natural law that could govern behaviour based simply on the natural urge for human self-preservation? Could human virtue be attained just through human reason in a new age of intellectual achievement? Were there foundational natural rights inherent in humankind that could provide a framework for justice and good governance?

Although the quest for answers to these questions initially sought to integrate the truths of Scripture with new philosophical thinking, this was without doubt the gestation period of modern secular humanism.

At last, it was OK to think for yourself

The foundations of humanism, applying human rationality to everything, including religious practice, go back at least to the Greek Stoics of antiquity, but the concepts gained significant impetus in the centuries before the Enlightenment through Christian writers such as Thomas Aquinas in the 13th century, and then Desiderius Erasmus, Martin Luther and John Calvin at the time of the Protestant Reformation. Their humanist thinking was not intended to replace God's commands in the Bible but to give further substance and validity to biblical truth through the rational capabilities of the human mind which God had created. These significant Christian thinkers promoted human reasoning alongside divine revelation. In fact, they argued that careful observance of the natural world could itself give certainty to the very existence of God.

They believed that it was not healthy to walk in blind faith to the dictates of the church hierarchy, not least because of the widespread superstition and corruption so clearly evident in much of the priesthood. Many Christian humanists believed that God had placed within humankind a sense of morality and justice, an inherent natural law, which He could bring to perfection and fulfilment through faith in Jesus Christ.

Influenced by Erasmus, Luther's strong challenge to the wrongful control of church and state was a huge step in the promotion of religious freedom in Europe. He stated in his writing on *Secular Authority* (1523):

> *Belief or unbelief is a matter of every one's conscience...*
> *Secular power... should permit men to believe one thing*
> *or another as they are able or willing, and constrain no*
> *one by force.*

By this, he was declaring not so much a basic human *right* of belief but a God-given human *ability* to choose belief, which no-one should presume to be able to take away. In reality, a Christian can be constrained by the state, if it so chooses, from voicing or expressing belief, but the heart choice of a believer cannot be overruled by another person, even when threatened with death.

Interestingly, it seems that there has often been some confusion in the minds of those promoting the ideology of human rights between what people have an *ability* to do and what they have a *right* to do. Followers of Jesus would say that God has given humankind the ability to do many things, including, sadly, many sinful things, but this does not mean that we have a God-given right or license to do these things.

For example, I have the ability to take my own life, but God has not conferred any right on me to carry out such an act. Some parents may claim a right to abort their unborn child, but this is only an ability, not an entitlement from God. To justify my wrongful actions by saying that I have a fundamental human right is to misunderstand the meaning of true delegated rights; they cannot be legitimately self-proclaimed, simply on the basis of ability.

Some of the Enlightenment thinkers and just a little of what they thought

Following these early seeds sown by writers such as Luther, many European philosophers during the 17th and 18th centuries developed humanist theories on the condition of man and his place in society. They had a profound influence on the burgeoning ideology of human rights. Here are some of the more significant contributors:

Hugo Grotius (1583–1645), born in Holland, has been described as the father of natural law, a concept of inherent ethical values arising from the inevitable desire of every human being for both self-preservation and the need to be part of society. Hugo Grotius concluded that an innate sense of right and wrong would exist even without the existence of God.

Thomas Hobbes (1588–1679), born in England, was not at all happy with organised religion and even less happy with the idea of the divine right of kings. This was the time of the

English civil war, when growing opposition to the absolutism of monarchy led to the beheading of Charles I. There was a desire to move on from the oppressive authority of state and church towards a new order that respected the voice and rights of the people. However, Hobbes was suspicious of democracy and he argued that unlimited pursuit of individual rights would simply lead to a world of unbounded fear and chaos.

Recognising the sinful nature of man, Hobbes advocated the need for a limited surrender of individual rights in submission to the ruling authority, in the form of a contract between the king and his subjects, to provide protection for both. He maintained that, without the consent of the people, the king could have no authority, and without this authority, even sometimes using coercive power, there could be no peace. The concept of an agreement of duties and entitlements between a ruler and those ruled became increasingly accepted, under the title of a *social contract*.

Descartes (1596–1650), born in France, is seen by many historians as a significant catalyst for the process of the Enlightenment in Europe. He maintained that everything had to be judged by human reason, and he is well known for concise statements such as 'The only thing that I cannot doubt is the fact that I doubt,' and 'I think therefore I am.' For Descartes, the individual self was the ultimate reference point in thought, giving a new licence for the emergence of powerful new ideologies of individualism and rationalism. Belief in the wisdom of man was now beginning to take precedence in European philosophy over the wisdom of God.

John Lilburne (1614–1657), born in England, was also writing during the time of the English civil war. He was a Puritan and later a Quaker, who found himself at odds with both the monarchy and with Oliver Cromwell's military dictatorship. In his writings, we see for the first time a clearly stated belief that there exists for every human being basic rights, which he called *freeborn rights*. He maintained that everyone was born with these fundamental rights, which were of particular relevance when facing legal disputes. He argued that these foundational rights were different from any entitlements conferred on citizens by statutes of governments. This was an important moment in the story of human rights because we see here the espousing of certain innate rights which were, in effect, considered to be God-given to every member of the human race, irrespective of their personal relationship with Him.

John Locke (1632–1704), born in England, has been described as the father of liberalism and the founder of the modern theory of human rights. Locke's ideas were strongly influenced by his opposition to the excesses of Charles II. Like Thomas Hobbes, he believed that those governing should only do so with the consent of those governed, and that rulers should acknowledge the existence of specific innate,

divinely ordained, natural rights for every human being. He named these as the right to life, to liberty and to ownership of possessions, and he was adamant that these foundational rights should not be surrendered in any social contract with those governing.

Locke believed that such rights needed to be grounded in man's duties to God. He maintained that a right to liberty should not be a right to self-indulgence; and he did not believe that human beings, as God's creatures, had a right to take their own lives. However, he seemed to assume that, in their pursuit of rights, all people could be constrained by a sense of Christian duty, ignoring the reality of innate carnality in every human being.

What became particularly relevant for those compiling the United States Declaration of Independence, some 100 years later, was the statement by Locke that people had a right of rebellion against those ruling, in the face of any tyrannical challenge to these foundational natural rights.

Francis Hutcheson (1694–1746), born in Ireland, was the Enlightenment philosopher who introduced the word *unalienable* or *inalienable* to the concept of rights, applying this description to those rights which, if infringed by government, would justify a right for the people to resist by force. The word *inalienable* implies that no attempt should be made to separate these named rights from any individual. It is important to note that it was this particular word that Thomas Jefferson used in justifying certain God-given rights in his composition of the United States Declaration of Independence. However, Francis Hutcheson also saw some conflict between promotion of these personal rights and what he called the *greatest public good*.

Jean-Jacques Rousseau (1712–1778), born in Switzerland, was a philosopher and the author of an important book called *The Social Contract*. Rousseau and Locke both advocated the need for a legally defined contract between those governing and those governed, detailing the distribution of rights and responsibilities of both sides for the common good. Like Hutcheson, he saw the conflict between personal freedom and submission to the needs of society as a whole. This inevitable competition, between the rights of individuals and the rights of society, remains a fundamental dilemma for lawmakers when the issue of sin is side-lined.

Importantly, Rousseau maintained that, rather than there being a divine arbiter over a nation's affairs, the expression of the general will of the people should be the only legitimate foundation for the establishing of government, morality and laws. With the help of education, he believed that this corporate will would be motivated by the desire of all citizens to improve their own wellbeing. The writings of Locke and Rousseau had a particularly significant influence in the following century on American independence and the French Revolution, and the subsequent declarations and constitutions which became established in those nations.

Mary Wollstonecraft (1759–1797), born in England, was furious at the views of Edmund Burke, an English politician, in his *Reflections on the Revolution in France,* a book in which he was very critical of the ideologies supporting the revolution. As a result, Mary Wollstonecraft published *A Vindication of the Rights of Men,* and later her more famous work, *A Vindication of the Rights of Women,* on account of which she has inevitably been seen by many as an early inspiration for the feminist movement of more recent times.

It is interesting to note the words written by Sir Roger Scruton in an article for the *Guardian* newspaper in May 2013, entitled *Identity, Marriage, Family: Our Core Conservative Values Have Been Betrayed:*

> *Our situation today mirrors that faced by [Edmund] Burke. Now, as then, abstract ideas and utopian schemes threaten to displace practical wisdom from political process. Instead of the common law of England we have the abstract idea of human rights, slapped upon us by European courts...*

I have included a number of quotes by Sir Roger Scruton in this book because his comments on the issue of rights are given more from a rational than religious standpoint. Despite this, he clearly describes the unsafe nature of a justice system based on the promotion of human rights, instead of one based on traditional biblical precepts.

Thomas Paine (1737–1809), born in England, further explored the idea of natural rights and the social contract. In his work, *Rights of Man* (which was also a strident response to Edmund Burke's condemnation of the French Revolution), he wrote that only by declaring and maintaining individual, natural rights could every citizen enter into a national contract to form a legitimate government. In another well-known book, *The Age of Reason*, Thomas Paine made very clear his belief that, in the light of unprecedented human intellectual advancement, ultimate sovereignty in all creation should rest with man rather than with God.

Paine was a friend of Benjamin Franklin and a strong supporter of the independence of America from British rule. He saw both monarchy and church hierarchy as inherently corrupt and, like John Locke, maintained that people had a right to overthrow any government that undermined their fundamental rights. He was quarrelsome and anti-Christian, describing himself, rather strangely, as a secular Quaker, and he ended his days in a sad place of poverty and disillusionment, having separated from two wives during his lifetime.

So what did all this Enlightenment thinking do for human rights?

There were huge steps forward in intellectual and scientific understanding during the period of the Enlightenment in Europe. There were also very significant and valuable challenges to the tyranny and corruption of both the state and the church. However, the Age of Reason increasingly encouraged the elevation of man's wisdom above the wisdom of God and the truths of the Bible. Modern secular humanism was birthed and given increasing validity alongside traditional Christianity.

The concept of rights for every person was fuelled by this humanism, resulting in a growing rejection of any role for God in the rule over nations. The general will of the people was now to be the driver of law, morality and government, setting aside the biblical notion of any divine delegation of authority affecting the affairs of man.

Everyone must obey state authorities, because no authority exists without God's permission, and the existing authorities have been put there by God. Romans 13:1 (GNT)

Personal natural rights were closely associated with the theory of natural law. This was a belief in self-evident norms of ethical behaviour, not prescribed by religious teaching or government statute but existing primarily out of mankind's natural urge for self-preservation. Surely, it was argued, a right to life and liberty for every human being was a foundational and very reasonable ethical principle, for promoting the wellbeing of humankind. But the Bible has a warning:

There is a way that seems right to a man, but its end is the way of death. Proverbs 14:12

Dissatisfied with the oppressive dictates of monarchy and church, many Enlightenment thinkers believed that natural rights or, as they were to become, universal human rights, could be adopted into the constitution of a nation, and so become a basis for ensuring justice for every citizen. We shall see later that this theory of self-evident, inalienable rights reached two historic and strategic milestones in the United States Declaration of Independence in 1776 and in the French Declaration of the Rights of Man in 1789.

The word *inalienable* became frequently attached to the concept of man's rights, adding apparent authenticity to the ideology by implying that such entitlements should be incapable of separation from any individual, either by government or any other human entity. It is worth noting, however, that even from the beginning of the debate on the existence of the rights of man, there was also a strong voice, albeit a minority, arguing that to describe humans as having such inalienable entitlements was meaningless or, at the very least, in contradiction to the much more important concept of human responsibility. They asked the question, "If an individual's rights were truly inalienable, how or when could it ever be acceptable to curtail those rights, even when seemingly necessary for the common good?" Many argued that such rights could not be supported by either self-evidence or natural law, but rather that the concept was simply the result of an evolving process of humanistic reasoning.

The fundamental issue of sovereignty in a nation

The question as to where governmental sovereignty should lie within a nation became an increasingly important issue during the Enlightenment. The interrelationship between sovereignty and rights is profound, because to self-proclaim a right that has not been conferred is to claim sovereignty. We shall see that this became a critical aspect of the ideological basis of the French Revolution. It is important to realise that political sovereignty will always reflect spiritual sovereignty. In other words, if the citizens of a nation, in their pursuance of an equitable society, declare that they are not accountable to any higher authority, they have contradicted the Word of God and given opportunity for the enemy's spiritual intrusion. The Bible does not say that all authority on earth should ultimately rest in the will of the people, but rather that all authority in heaven and earth has been created through, and exists for, the Son of God.

For through him God created everything in heaven and on earth, the seen and the unseen things, including spiritual powers, lords, rulers, and authorities. God created the whole universe through him and for him. Colossians 1:16 (GNT)

When the sovereignty of God is ignored, there is a hiatus of spiritual authority and, whether people understand it or not, they are left vulnerable and confused as to where ultimate authority lies. Deep within the human spirit, it feels unsafe for such sovereignty to lie with created humans rather than the Creator. Secular humanism has left mankind with precisely this sense of insecurity, which can never be resolved by pursuing the notion of self-evident rights. We shall look further at the issue of sovereignty in a later chapter.

The Enlightenment Period and the loss of true Light

Biblical revelation and the need for a direct relationship with God seemed, to many, increasingly irrelevant. The Age of Enlightenment was seen as an escape from the straitjacket of conventional Christian dogma and superstition, a celebration of reason over blind religious obedience. Surely, it was argued, men and women could improve their lives through the recognition of human potential and scientific discovery rather than through the Church. Erasmus Darwin, a key Enlightenment thinker, derided Christianity and was very forthright in his evolutionary ideas, strongly declaring that human lives are not fixed by God. Not surprising then that his grandson, Charles Darwin, wrote his revolutionary book *On the Origin of Species*, proposing an evolutionary origin for mankind in clear denial of the creation narrative of the Bible.

The Age of Enlightenment in Europe was, in many ways, a time of marked progress in scientific rigour and the abandoning of countless superstitious beliefs, in the quest for new thinking and freedom from religious oppression. Sadly, however, the true source of spiritual light was largely lost. Man's intellect was seen as negating the need for God's truth, and much of Europe forgot the need for Jesus Christ.

In Him was life, and the life was the Light of men. The Light shines in the darkness, and the darkness did not comprehend it. John 1:4–5

In summary

Church reformers such as Luther, with his demands for personal freedom of religious conscience for each person, helped to open a door to finding release from the oppressive rule of church and state. Some simply wanted to bring more human reason into their Christian experience, rather than the mindless following of religious practice. Some looked for better ways of establishing a just relationship between the monarch, parliament and people. As the Enlightenment progressed, the revelation of truth through the Bible seemed an obsolete idea, as science appeared to be providing so many answers to life's mysteries.

In the search for new ways of defining human morality and justice, the concept of natural rights – universal human entitlements irrespective of any relationship with God – became increasingly popular. By the last few decades of the 18th century this ideology had grown to be the focus of a strong political movement, which regarded the inalienable rights of man as of paramount importance and a powerful justification for rebelling against unwanted rule and rulers.

Chapter 4

Rights Take Centre-Stage

Independence and rights

In 1776, exasperated by unjust colonial rule, the original 13 American states took a stand against Great Britain, and King George III in particular, and declared their independence. Although not an unreasonable aspiration, the justification for what was, in fact, an act of rebellion, took full advantage of John Locke's writings on personal liberty, not least his maintaining of the right of rebellion against tyrannical government.

Christianity has clearly been hugely significant and beneficial in shaping the justice systems of the United States of America, and every president except Barack Obama has described the country as a Christian nation. However, the statements made during the strategic moment of independence, whilst giving voice to important Christian principles, were also strongly influenced by Enlightenment thinking.

Starting as a slow protest movement, then encouraged by Thomas Paine's book *Common Sense*, the decision was made to demand independence from the British Crown. Thomas Jefferson (a deist and philosophical writer), Benjamin Franklin (a polymath and Freemason) and George Washington (a practical soldier and influential landowner) masterminded the now famous Declaration of Independence. They combined biblical precepts with the views of Enlightenment writers and Freemasons from Europe, even taking advantage of a popular revival, notably among Scottish writers, in a philosophy called Epicureanism. This argued that the purpose of life, and indeed man's entitlement, was essentially the pursuit of pleasure or happiness. Jefferson embraced this notion, combining it with Hutcheson's arguments on the inalienability of certain rights, to give a framework for the wording of the declaration.

The Preamble essentially stated the reason for the overthrow of the British governing authorities, pointing out the unreasonable demands of the British monarchy. The reference to foundational rights was intended to provide the philosophical and indeed divine justification that Jefferson, and the fifty-five other signatories, needed in order to persuade the American people that this rebellion was morally acceptable.

The wording of the Preamble to the Declaration is of particular importance to our study of the historical progress of the ideology of rights. Let's look again at what it states:

> *We hold these truths to be self-evident, that all men are created equal, that they are endowed by their Creator with certain unalienable Rights, that among these are Life, Liberty and the Pursuit of Happiness.*

This is a profound claim. It is saying that there are two foundational truths, but it fails to provide any supporting evidence of validity, except to say that these truths are apparently *self-evident*. In fact, the first stated self-evident truth, concerning equality, finds good evidence in the Word of God. The Bible repeatedly declares that God sees all human beings as being of equal value, quantified, one might say, by the payment of Jesus in His death on the Cross for every person.

For God loved the world so much that he gave his only Son, so that everyone who believes in him may not die but have eternal life. John 3:16 (GNT)

However, it is important to clarify here that, although the Bible's definition of human equality attributes the same value to every human being irrespective of background, belief or behaviour, the Bible nowhere implies that every belief, behaviour or lifestyle is equally acceptable to God.

The second stated truth in the Preamble, namely that God has endowed humankind with certain unalienable rights, also apparently self-evident, finds no support either in the Bible nor in common sense. It is neither true nor even logical that God would choose, irrespective of any relationship with Him, to confer onto every human being entitlements or rights which they can apparently demand without obedience to any divine requirement of behaviour or lifestyle.

Thomas Jefferson may have viewed a God-given endowment of inalienable rights to life, liberty and the pursuit of happiness as requiring no further evidence, and he may have believed such conferral as wholly reasonable, but nowhere in the Bible is there any endorsement of this statement. Indeed, according to the Word of God, the sinfulness of mankind means they deserve death rather than life (Romans 6:23), bondage rather than freedom (Proverbs 5:22) and distress rather than happiness (Zephaniah 1:17).

The plausibility of any concept, such as that of universal human rights, does not ensure that it is either valid or valuable; good ideas are frequently not God's ideas. In fact, I believe that we are seeing at this key moment in history the birth of a new man-made religion, which is founded on a false assumption that claiming divine impartation of entitlement to every human being is the true pathway to justice for both the individual and for nations. We can say that the new religion of the *rights of man* is at this point openly challenging the biblical truth of a need to resolve the *sins of man*.

Interestingly, the Declaration of Independence concludes with a further invoking of divine approval for the concept of inalienable rights:

> *We, therefore, the Representatives of the United States of America, in General Congress, assembled, appealing to the Supreme Judge of the world for the rectitude of our intentions, do in the name, and by the authority of the good people of these colonies, solemnly publish and declare, that these United Colonies are, and of right ought to be, free and independent states...*

This seeking of endorsement, by the so-called *Supreme Judge of the world*, to a human declaration of man's entitlements will be repeated in a similar way, as we shall see later, in the revolutionary activities in France during the next decade.

The Bill of Rights
After the leaders of the newly independent United States wrote the Constitution, they had to get the agreement of all the thirteen

states, but some of the states didn't want to agree unless they could add some specific amendments, in the form of safeguards or rights for the people. So, in 1791 the United States added ten new articles to the Constitution. This document is called the *Bill of Rights*. It is interesting to see how the language of rights became so significant in the politics of the day in seeking to restrict unjust governmental control. This document was primarily intended to form part of the social contract between the new government and the people, but once the word *right* is used, it seems that it invariably takes on a quasi-religious significance in the minds of the participants. Entitlements intended simply to form a working political contract can become entrenched in people's minds as being something akin to a divinely imparted birthright.

It is worth just taking a moment to look at one of the clauses of the Bill of Rights, the Second Amendment. I suggest that here is a good example of an entitlement causing more strife than peace when a simple constitutional right, given to the people at a particular time of need, has progressively taken on the status of a religious right, and is guarded by many with equal fervour.

The Second Amendment of the American Bill of Rights says:

> *A well-regulated Militia, being necessary to the security of a free State, the right of the people to keep and bear arms shall not be infringed.*

At the time of writing this book, there has just been another horrible mass shooting at a school in America. Many people, including the president, are saying that there must be stronger gun control. However, there is a very powerful lobby demanding the absolute right to keep and bear arms in accordance with the Second Amendment detailed above. This demand is made despite the fact that the amendment was originally intended to provide for corporate rather than individual defence, needed prior to the formation of full-time security forces. The extraordinary strength with which this particular right is guarded by many, including Christians, shows just how deeply entrenched these entitlements can become in people's hearts.

Revolution and rights

We come now to a hugely significant spiritual episode in European history. In just a few years France underwent a seismic and strategic transformation, as traditional assumptions of church and state hierarchy were completely replaced by Enlightenment principles, promoting the sovereignty of the nation's citizens and the inalienable rights of each man. British author Thomas Carlyle, in his book *The French Revolution: A History,* says that it resulted from "the financial bankruptcy of the nation on the back of spiritual bankruptcy, and triggered by famine." He further described it as "open, violent rebellion, and victory, of dis-imprisoned anarchy against corrupt worn-out authority."

In constituting a new structure for French society, the revolutionary mood of 1789 required omission of any clear reference to the God of the Bible. The foundational document for this new order, entitled The Declaration of the Rights of Man and of the Citizen, was stated to have been drafted *under the auspices of the Supreme Being,* a name not found in Scripture but closely associated with Freemasonry. Indeed, many of the instigators of the French revolution, which aggressively brought about the removal of the monarchy and the rejection of church authority, were Freemasons. It is important to remember that Freemasons have a complex mixture of occult, deism and dualism in their literature, which noticeably avoids any reference to the tripartite nature of the biblical Godhead.

French kings had actually regarded themselves as fathers of the people, anointed by God to serve the nation, with powers limited by statute, but corruption had been all too obvious and increasingly intolerable for the populace. In addition, the people were let down by the church, damaged by the government's financial mismanagement and finally broken by shortage of food.

In the midst of the bitter struggles of the revolution, and following the famous assault on the Bastille, a prison representative to many of the tyranny of state authority, the strategic document *The Rights of Man* was drawn up by the Marquis de Lafayette, reflecting many of the radical views of the Enlightenment. For the first time in European history the concept of inalienable human rights was embedded into the constitution of a nation.

The Marquis had been associated with Thomas Jefferson and the United States Declaration of Independence, and now, in the upheaval of the French Revolution, the belief in natural and inalienable human rights became the cornerstone of a new system of justice in a European country. The quest for freedom from oppressive authority had come a long way from Luther to Lafayette, a journey from belief in the need for liberty of religious conscience to a belief in freedom through claiming innate human entitlement; a journey from a God-centred justice system, founded on the resolving of sin, to a man-centred system founded in the declaring of rights.

State sponsorship of the new religion of rights

The preamble to this strategic declaration states the following (bold added):

> *The Representatives of the French people, organised in the National Assembly, considering that ignorance, forgetfulness, or* **contempt of the rights of man are the sole cause of public miseries** *and the corruption of governments, have resolved to set forth in a solemn declaration the natural,* **inalienable, and sacred rights of man,** *so this declaration, being ever present to all the members of the social body, may unceasingly remind them of their rights and duties; in order that the acts of legislative power, may at each moment be compared with the aim of every political institution and thereby may be more respected; and in order that the demands of the citizens, grounded henceforth upon simple and* **incontestable principles,** *may always take the direction of maintaining the constitution and welfare of all.* **In consequence, the National Assembly recognizes and declares, in the presence and under the auspices of the Supreme Being, the following rights of man and citizen.**

We see here that faith has completely switched from God, as being the answer to man's distressed condition (*public miseries*), to a dependence on the new religion of the rights of man. According to the Bible, man's sin is the sole cause of his misery. God could not have given a clearer explanation to His covenant people, the Children of Israel: man's contempt for the commands of God is what has led to all the disorder and dysfunction of this world.

> *"But if you disobey the LORD your God and do not faithfully keep all his commands and laws that I am giving you today, all these evil things will happen to you." Deuteronomy 28:15 (GNT)*

There are further significant statements contained within this strategic preamble. It describes the rights of man, which are subsequently listed in the declaration, as *inalienable*, *sacred*, and based upon *incontestable principles*. Clearly, these rights must never be taken away from French citizens, must be defended with religious zeal, and must never be challenged as being invalid. This new religion of rights certainly does not allow dissenters.

And what about this *Supreme Being* who is given the right to oversee this momentous declaration? Who is it? The Bible does not recognise this title for God. In fact, the name is an intended denial of the Trinity of Father, Son and Holy Spirit, and therefore, according to scripture, it must refer to an antichrist spirit.

Who is the liar but the one who denies that Jesus is the Christ? This is the antichrist, the one who denies the Father and the Son. 1 John 2:22

This demonic power, *The Supreme Being,* can only be part of the dominion of the ruler of the world, Satan, whom Jesus, thankfully, utterly refused to serve.

"All this will be yours, then, if you worship me." Jesus answered, "The scripture says, 'Worship the Lord your God and serve only him!'" Luke 4:7–8 (GNT)

The new man-made religion of human rights, birthed into the world through the American Declaration of Independence, has now grown into a state-sponsored creed, in the midst of the French Revolution.

Ditching the Ten Commandments
It is important to note that a contemporary artist's depiction of this declaration (now at the Musée Carnavalet in Paris) shows

the seventeen articles written onto stone tablets very similar to the traditional depiction of the setting of the Ten Commandments.

There can be no doubt as to the intentions of the artist, and of those who commissioned the work: the newly declared rights of the citizens of France were to be seen as replacing God's commandments of the Bible.

It also confirms that the spiritual oversight of this new foundation of justice was not to be the God of the Bible but a human-constructed deity, shown in the painting as an all-seeing eye (an occult symbol used in Freemasonry) watching over the newly declared rights. The symbolism of this well-known picture was in fact a very powerful proclamation of the spiritual reality of the enemy's new rule over the constitutional and justice systems of France.

Ditching the truths of the bible

We will look at a few of the articles of this declaration to see how there is a consistent denial of biblical truth in favour of a rights-based humanist ideology.

Article 1: Men are born free and remain free.

The Bible disagrees. We inherit the bondage of sin and iniquity at conception from the sin of our ancestors. King David and Jeremiah were well aware of this.

> *I have been evil from the day I was born; from the time I was conceived, I have been sinful. Psalm 51:5 (GNT)*

Our ancestors sinned, but now they are gone, and we are suffering for their sins. Lamentations 5:7 (GNT)

Jesus makes it clear where bondage truly comes from, and it is only through Him that we can find freedom from this inherited and ongoing problem.

Jesus said to them, "I am telling you the truth: everyone who sins is a slave of sin." John 8:34 (GNT)

For you know what was paid to set you free from the worthless manner of life handed down by your ancestors. It was not something that can be destroyed, such as silver or gold; it was the costly sacrifice of Christ, who was like a lamb without defect or flaw. 1 Peter 1:18–19 (GNT)

Article 2: Man's natural and imprescriptible rights are liberty, property, security, and resistance to oppression.
The Bible disagrees. The world may choose to believe in, and legislate for, such natural rights that are imprescriptible (cannot be taken away), but the ways of God's Kingdom are radically different from this world-view of entitlement. Jesus does not say that we have a natural right to liberty unless we deal with sin through obedience to Him.

If the Son sets you free, then you will be really free. John 8:36 (GNT)

Jesus does not say that in His Kingdom we have a natural right to property.

Sell all your belongings and give the money to the poor. Provide for yourselves purses that don't wear out, and save your riches in heaven, where they will never decrease, because no thief can get to them, and no moth can destroy them. Luke 12:33 (GNT)

For you showed sympathy to the prisoners and accepted joyfully the seizure of your property, knowing that you have for yourselves a better possession and a lasting one. Hebrews 10:34

Jesus does not say that we have a natural right to security, but rather that we can find perfect safety in Him from the Evil One.

"I am the good shepherd, who is willing to die for the sheep." John 10:11 (GNT)

Jesus does not say that in His Kingdom we have a natural right to resist oppression.

"And if one of the occupation troops forces you to carry his pack one mile, carry it two miles." Matthew 5:41 (GNT)

Article 3: The source of all sovereignty resides essentially in the nation.

The Bible disagrees. It is very clear where the source of all authority lies, both spiritual and temporal, and to whom it has been given.

Jesus drew near and said to them, "I have been given all authority in heaven and on earth." Matthew 28:18 (GNT)

Everyone must obey state authorities, because no authority exists without God's permission, and the existing authorities have been put there by God. Romans 13:1 (GNT)

Article 4: Liberty consists in the power to do anything that does not injure others.
This is a foundational tenet of secular humanism, appearing to be so very reasonable. I should surely be able to do whatever I wish so long as it does not affect anyone else. The problem is that sin affects not just the one who sins but all those who come in contact with that person, particularly those for whom the sinner carries a measure of responsibility. It has been rightly said that personal sin frequently pollutes the public water supply.

> *But because they [the Levites] conducted the worship of idols for the people of Israel and in this way led the people into sin, I, the Sovereign LORD, solemnly swear that they must be punished. Ezekiel 44:12 (GNT)*

Article 6: The law should be the expression of the general will.
The Bible disagrees with these enlightenment ideas of Rousseau and others. If justice depends merely on the corporate will in the hearts of the people, then deception can be the only outcome.

> *The heart is more deceitful than all else and is desperately sick; who can understand it? Jeremiah 17:9*

God has explained and demonstrated the laws of His creation which will bring well-being to humankind, written down under the Old Covenant, and then fulfilled through Jesus under the New Covenant.

> *God gave the Law through Moses, but grace and truth came through Jesus Christ. John 1:17 (GNT)*

Revolutionary results
Perhaps the most profound spiritual statement is made in Article 3, mentioned above:

> *The principle of all sovereignty resides essentially in the nation. No body nor individual may exercise any authority which does not proceed directly from the nation.*

Although a very understandable response to the corrupt practices of monarchy, church and government, this statement had huge spiritual as well as political consequences. Sovereignty is a position of authority where there is no accountability to another. When the French people self-declared the rights of man and, in effect, laid claim to ultimate political and spiritual sovereignty, in denying the overall authority of the God of the Bible, they lost the means of His protection and correction, and opened a door to anarchy.

In 1790, the British politician Edmund Burke warned of bloody and violent consequences to what was happening in France. The tensions between the liberal and monarchist factions of the revolution finally resulted in a republic being declared in 1792, and in King Louis XVI being executed the following year. What followed this rejection of divine order were the years referred to by historians as the *Reign of Terror*. It was a time of gross lawlessness and the death of tens of thousands of French citizens at the guillotine, while eloquent and charismatic political leaders vied to demonstrate to the populace their revolutionary fervour.

One of the more extreme leaders arising out of the spiritual confusion of the revolution was Maximilien Robespierre, who even tried, briefly, to initiate a new state religion, worshipping two deities named *Supreme Being* and *Reason*. The widespread fanatical desire to replace biblical principles even led to a proposal for a ten-day week, but thankfully, this did not catch on. The violence continued unabated until Robespierre himself was executed, and some form of national stability was only restored when a Consulate was formed in 1799 under Napoleon Bonaparte. He was an extraordinarily strong and charismatic leader, who brilliantly camouflaged his own will by giving the impression of following the general will of the people.

The government in Britain at the time looked on mostly in horror and in fear of similar unrest at home. The Prime Minister, William Pitt the Younger, commented in a parliamentary speech, "We see, therefore, that France has trampled underfoot all laws, human and divine." Also in a speech, Edmund Burke was even more critical of the Revolution, declaring, "The French had shewn themselves the ablest architects of ruin that had hitherto existed in the world. In that very short space of time they had completely pulled down to the ground, their monarchy; their church; their nobility; their law; their revenue; their army; their navy; their commerce; their arts; and their manufactures…"

In a 1989 essay, *Man's Second Disobedience*, the philosopher Sir Roger Scruton wrote:

> *By proclaiming a purely abstract 'Liberty', the French Revolution facilitated the destruction of the qualified and partial liberties which come through the work of compromise. By offering abstract Rights, it legitimised the destruction of law.*

The gods of pride and humanism replace the God of the Bible

There is no doubt that both the church and the state in France had become seriously corrupt in the years preceding the revolution, but God's way of tackling such corruption is to challenge the sin of those in authority, not to destroy all the administrative structures of society. Some changes were, of course, for the better, as the dignity and merit of every citizen was given considerably more value. But we need once again to remember that the promotion of innate rights is very different from the promotion of innate value.

It was not long before Napoleon, an even more despotic ruler than the monarchy which the revolution had overthrown, decided to call himself a constitutional king and then later an emperor. Interestingly, at the moment of Napoleon's crowning, in 1804, he pointedly took the crown from the Pope and placed it on his own head, discounting any authority above his own. He was emphasising that his position was by his own merit and by the will of the people and did not require religious conferral or consecration. One might say that God was permitted to be in attendance, and to endorse Napoleon's crowning, but He was not permitted to be the source of this declared sovereignty.

As well as being a pivotal moment in promoting the ideology of universal rights, many historians see the French Revolution, and the events that followed, as a key step for modern secular humanism in Europe, the sovereignty of man openly replacing the sovereignty of God in a national context. Although a Concordat, signed by Napoleon and the Pope in 1801, brought a measure of reconciliation with the Church in France, the church-state balance of relationship remained tilted very firmly in Napoleon's favour. He understood the utility of religion as a useful tool for social cohesion, but it was to be kept strictly under his control. There are, perhaps, parallels to this approach existing in many nations today.

It is interesting to reflect on the spiritual door that was opened by the denial of divine sovereignty, and the resulting megalomania of Napoleon in regard to his plans for the whole of Europe. He is quoted as saying to his secretary:

> *There must be a superior power which dominates all other powers, with enough authority to force them to live in harmony with one another, and France is the best placed for that purpose. We must have a European legal system, a European appeal court, a common currency, the same weights and measures, the same laws.*

It seems that Napoleon was exhibiting a spirit very similar to that which operated in the ancient king of Babylon, a spirit given licence both in Babylon and in France by these particular rulers claiming a right to be like God.

You were determined to climb up to heaven and to place your throne above the highest stars. You thought you would sit like a king on that mountain in the north where the gods assemble. You said you would climb to the tops of the clouds and be like the Almighty. Isaiah 14:13–14 (GNT)

In summary

In the growing revolutionary climate towards the end of the Period of the Enlightenment, encouraged by writers such as John Locke and Thomas Paine, a strategic document was drawn up in the United States in 1776 in support of independence from British rule. In this Declaration, it was stated that there was a significant and self-evident truth, namely that humankind had been endowed by the Creator with certain inalienable rights, to life, liberty and the pursuit of happiness, irrespective of a personal relationship with God.

Despite this assertion being biblically untrue, it became a pivotal moment in the international promotion of the ideology of human rights, soon to be powerfully encouraged and reinforced with a religious zeal during the French Revolution.

We can say that, from this time, worldwide justice systems started a radical journey towards a new and experimental faith, the religion of human rights, progressively replacing the concepts of right and wrong given in the Bible.

Copied and extended by many politicians since that time, The Rights of Man and the Citizen, drafted in 1789, was a strategic document in world history. For the first time, in Europe at least, the humanistic concept of inalienable rights was written into the constitution of a nation while, at the same time, God's authority over the nation was written out. All subsequent national and international declarations of human rights have built upon that precedent.

Chapter 5

International Assent to the Religion of Rights

The world was desperate to find a new way of justice

In 1948, the year that the nation of Israel was re-established, following a devastating world war and the Jewish holocaust, the United Nations General Assembly adopted The Universal Declaration of Human Rights, intended as a worldwide bulwark against extremes of oppression and discrimination. Drafted with the best of intentions, it was, in many ways, a landmark attainment in world history, bringing together many nations in a search for justice and peace. It sought to unite many conflicting political, religious and cultural systems into one agreement regarding human morality, dignity and rights.

Picking up the wording of both the United States Declaration of Independence and the French Declaration of the Rights of Man, the preamble to this new declaration stated the basic principle behind the document:

> *[In] recognition of the inherent dignity and of the equal and inalienable rights of all members of the human family [that are] the foundation of freedom, justice and peace in the world...*

Once again, this statement, although a perfectly reasonable proposal, does not agree with God's Word. Humankind may not like the concept of sin, but the Bible says clearly that it is the sinfulness of man that is the sole reason for the absence of freedom, justice and peace in the world. Nehemiah heard of the distress of God's people in Jerusalem and wept over their condition, and the reproach of neighbouring peoples.

They told me that those who had survived and were back in the homeland were in great difficulty and that the foreigners who lived nearby looked down on them. Nehemiah 1:3a (GNT)

Nehemiah knew the cause of their troubles. It had nothing to do with the recognition and claiming of inalienable rights but everything to do with unconfessed sin.

Look at me, LORD, and hear my prayer, as I pray day and night for your servants, the people of Israel. I confess that we, the people of Israel, have sinned. My ancestors and I have sinned. Nehemiah 1:6 (GNT)

Although by 1948 the concept of inalienable human rights was entirely man-made, not intended to rest on religious precepts, the whole declaration was, in reality, an act of faith in secular humanism, and the ideology of rights in particular. The preamble goes on to say (bold added):

> *The peoples of the United Nations have in the Charter **reaffirmed their faith** in fundamental human rights...*

Justice by declaring man's rights rather than what God says is right

Article 3 of the declaration clarifies what these fundamental rights are now deemed to be:

> *Everyone has the right to life, liberty and security of person.*

Again, we can say that, in the absence of the truth of God's Word, this statement is not unreasonable, but for the Body of Christ it is important that we recognize the clear differences between this human view of justice and the ways of God's Kingdom. We are *in* the world but our heart attitudes should not be *of* it. The world says that the right to life and liberty for every human being is surely indisputable.

However, as we have already noted, the Bible does not say that unredeemed man has a right to life, but rather that in Jesus alone is there fullness of life.

You have been given full life in union with him. He is supreme over every spiritual ruler and authority. Colossians 2:10 (GNT)

Jesus explains that sin not only steals eternal life but can steal earthly life.

"What about those eighteen people in Siloam who were killed when the tower fell on them? Do you suppose this proves that they were worse than all the other people living in Jerusalem? No indeed! And I tell you that if you do not turn from your sins, you will all die as they did." Luke 13:4–5 (GNT)

The Bible also explains that true personal liberty actually consists of knowing and responding to truth that is revealed through the Word of God and in being a disciple of Jesus Christ.

> *So Jesus said to those who believed in him, "If you obey my teaching, you are really my disciples; you will know the truth, and the truth will set you free." John 8:31–32 (GNT)*

The wisdom of man versus the wisdom of God

The ways of God's Kingdom are radically different from the ways of the world. God's view of our rights is very likely to contradict the perceived entitlements which man passionately believes are his due. It may seem a relatively trivial example, but let's consider Article 23 of this universal declaration, which says:

> *Everyone, without discrimination, has the right to equal pay for equal work.*

Jesus so often shocked His followers with how different the Kingdom of God is from the kingdoms of this world. As previously mentioned, the story of the vineyard workers made it clear that what God says is fair may well conflict with our sense of fairness. Equal reward for equal effort may make human sense, but God's boundless grace inevitably contradicts the wisdom of the world, and carnal man will not necessarily understand it when God says that His ways are what bring true peace to humankind. Jesus never encouraged His followers to proclaim, "What about my rights?" Instead He pointed them to the fact that God always knows what is fair and right:

*"And to those [the labourers hired throughout the day] he [the landowner] said, 'You also go into the vineyard, and **whatever is right I will give you.**'" Matthew 20:4 (bold added)*

The spiritual reality of universal rights

Although intended by those involved, including many Christians, to put an end to worldwide injustice and tyrannical control by governments, the 1948 declaration of human rights was, I suggest, a spiritually regressive document. It sealed the unbiblical ideology of innate rights into an international legal framework. Despite the laudable desire to promote human dignity, it steered justice systems away from a sound biblical foundation towards statutes clearly based on faith in secular humanism. Neither the God of the Bible nor any other deity was intentionally invoked as the source of these apparent rights in this twentieth-century version of the earlier declarations. Instead, human entitlement was now entirely self-proclaimed, apparently independent of any need for divine approval.

I have several times said that, for any rights to have legitimacy, they must be conferred by one who has greater authority. If I declare that I have a right to life, it begs the question of who has given me this right. In the United States in 1776, there was an attempt, albeit without a sound foundation, to invoke the authority of the Creator. In France in 1789, the Supreme Being, an Enlightenment deity, was declared to be the one who legitimised the declaration of the rights of man. As it happens, this proclaimed spiritual patronage over the French constitution was probably quite accurate, in that this document clearly gave considerable licence to the evil one that Jesus calls the ruler of the world.

By 1948, there was an international consensus, in order to avoid religious dispute, that no spiritual authority should be mentioned in this strategic document pursuing human wellbeing and justice. This declaration presumed that human beings should be able to determine their own duties and entitlements. In effect, the citizens of every nation were seen to be fully sovereign, both politically and spiritually. Of course, the intention was to unite people from many different cultural and religious backgrounds into one universal and acceptable answer to man's inhumanity to man, so deeply experienced during the Second World War. However, good intentions do not necessarily lead to spiritually sound results. It is interesting that this 1948 declaration has evolved, in the last half-century, into many documents which frequently incorporate the word *covenant*, a concept borrowed from the Bible. I suggest that enshrining the ideology of rights into covenantal agreements between nations only leads to this man-made religion giving even more licence to the god of this world. We shall explore the important relevance of covenant later.

Europe is converted to the new religion

From this very significant declaration in 1948, the ideology of rights gained considerable momentum. Recognising real oppression experienced by people groups and individuals, many governments began to affirm that the promotion of rights would be the best answer to seeking justice and freedom. Of course, it's reasonable that, in the relationship between a government and an individual citizen, each should sign up to a contract of reciprocal rights and duties, upheld by the rule of law. However, the faith now being placed in universal rights went well beyond a necessary social contract, to an ideology demanding, frequently with a religious zeal, adherence to a new code of international morality.

Very shortly after the 1948 declaration, in 1950, countries in Europe picked up the concept in the European Convention of Human Rights. The preamble to the document of this convention includes the following statements (bold added):

> *... Considering the Universal Declaration of Human Rights proclaimed by the General Assembly of the United Nations on 10th December 1948 ... Reaffirming their **profound belief in** those Fundamental Freedoms which are the foundation of justice and peace in the world and are best maintained ... by observance of the **Human Rights**... Being resolved ... to take the first steps for the **collective enforcement** of certain of the Rights.*

It is pertinent that this convention resolved to *enforce* the concepts associated with human rights within its jurisdiction. This new belief, in fact a new religion, not only received growing international recognition, but adherents have increasingly taken upon themselves the right to enforce their ideology by stringent laws. For example, under the United Kingdom Equality Act 2010, it is now illegal, albeit with certain exceptions, to refuse to endorse same-sex marriage through any withholding of the provision of goods and services.

The case of a Christian baker, who felt that providing a cake which promoted gay marriage would contradict his deeply held beliefs, has become notorious. In the UK, the right of any couple to promote their personal belief in *same-sex* marriage, through demanding a particular baker's services, must now inevitably compete with the baker's right to work according to his personal belief in *biblical* marriage. The enforcement of rights in Britain has indeed gone well beyond the necessary provision of entitlements and duties for an ordered society. It seems that rights ideology is now the dominant method of imposing liberal moral values on every citizen.

What about the American civil rights movement?

In the 1860's America fought a civil war over the issue of slavery. Many people at the time, including black activists such as Frederick Douglass, who had himself been a slave, spoke out for freedom and equality of citizenship for black Americans. Slavery was finally abolished in the United States in 1865, but much of the prejudice against the freed black slaves remained unresolved.

A hundred years later, during the 1960's, the African-American Civil Rights Movement highlighted the inequality between races. It inspired similar challenges to social injustice in other countries such as South Africa, but it was primarily intended to end racial segregation of black Americans in the United States, particularly in the southern states. The main thrust of this movement was not so much to claim the innate human rights of black Americans but rather to challenge deeply destructive social prejudice, in regard to the black community having equal citizens' rights through access to employment, schooling, politics etc. The issue was primarily about the innate value of every American, irrespective of race and colour, and the movement did eventually lead to a significant change in national attitudes.

The leaders organised major campaigns of protest and civil disobedience, which were for the most part non-violent, although later the Black Power Movement was more aggressive in its demands. The most significant individual of the civil rights movement at this time was Dr Martin Luther King, Jr., who won the 1964 Nobel Peace Prize for his role, but sadly was assassinated in 1968. His promotion of non-violent demonstrations against apartheid and poverty was founded in his Christian beliefs. He is particularly remembered for a speech given in Washington in 1963. Here is the most well-known part of that speech (bold added):

I say to you today, my friends, so even though we face the difficulties of today and tomorrow, I still have a dream. It is a dream deeply rooted in the American dream.

I have a dream that one day this nation will rise up and live out the true meaning of its creed: 'We hold these truths to be self-evident: that all men are created equal.'

I have a dream that one day on the red hills of Georgia the sons of former slaves and the sons of former slave owners will be able to sit down together at the table of brotherhood.

I have a dream that one day even the state of Mississippi, a state sweltering with the heat of injustice, sweltering with the heat of oppression, will be transformed into an oasis of freedom and justice.

I have a dream that my four little children will one day live in a nation where they will not be judged by the color of their skin but by the content of their character.

I have a dream today.
I have a dream that one day, down in Alabama, with its vicious racists, with its governor having his lips dripping with the words of interposition and nullification; one day right there in Alabama, little black boys and black girls will be able to join hands with little white boys and white girls as sisters and brothers.

I have a dream today.

It's important to note that King chose to highlight the God-ordained equality of man's innate value rather than the existence of God-given rights. He knew that the inalienable worth of every human being is biblical truth. God sees everyone, no matter what gender, status, ability, colour or race as being of equal and significant value. However, it is only in obedience to Him, through Jesus Christ, that a right is conferred by God for each of us to belong to His family. Sin does not destroy our worth in God's eyes, but it does destroy our ability to be in covenant relationship with Him and know our entitlements as His children.

For God loved the world so much that he gave his only Son, so that everyone who believes in him may not die but have eternal life. John 3:16 (GNT)

Is the United Nations now the universal arbiter of morality?

When, in November 2017, the United Nations Human Rights Committee chose to exclude unborn children from the right to life, no expert expressed concern for children in the womb being capable of feeling pain, nor did they bring up the Convention on the Rights of the Child, which expressly requires all nations to protect children before birth. The committee ignored the fact that the United States, Russia, Egypt, Japan, Poland, and others denied the committee's authority to read a right to abortion into the UN treaty on human rights.

Nothing demonstrates more clearly the foolishness of a justice system based on competing rights, as opposed to God's system based on acknowledging sin. The committee's decision simply brings into stark focus the inevitability of the opposing rights of the foetus and the mother. All scientists would agree that the first cell of a new and unique human life begins existence at the moment of fertilization when one living sperm from the father joins with one living ovum from the mother. So, the question for the UN committee must be, "When does a human life earn its so-called rights?"

Another UN Committee on the Rights of the Child recently wrote a report which contained 150 recommendations on matters where Britain could be contravening the UN's charter, including the right of children to receive confidential counselling and sexuality education, without the need for parental or legal guardian consent. Another recommendation made clear the committee's view that requiring children to attend Christian

assemblies undermines their human rights.

The unchanging Word and wisdom of God says that the wellbeing of mankind is secured when sinful behaviour is addressed, whether this is in the life of a child or an adult.

Children, obey your parents in the Lord, for this is right. Fathers, do not provoke your children to anger, but bring them up in the discipline and instruction of the Lord. Ephesians 6:1,4

In contrast to this, the ever-changing wisdom of man, voiced in decisions coming from the United Nations Human Rights Committees, is increasingly saying that wellbeing in the family is only achieved through declaring and enforcing the individual rights of parents and children. Sadly, this humanistic opinion-based morality will have the serious effect of dividing children from their parents. Thank God that His instructions draw families together by making it possible to deal with the sin that separates, and we are given a precious opportunity to find healing for the mistakes of the past.

At the time of writing, there seems to be a disproportionate focus in the United Nations on issues of sexuality, with considerable pressure coming particularly from France, the Netherlands, Canada and Spain. As an example, there are moves among a particular UN group of nine rapporteurs to promote adoption of the following statement, known as the Yogyakarta Principles:

> *The expression, practice and promotion of different opinions, convictions and beliefs, with regard to issues of sexual orientation or gender identity, should not be undertaken in a manner incompatible with human rights. [Consequently, there should be] no medical or psychological treatment or counselling to treat sexual orientation and gender identity as medical conditions.*

Such issues regarding sexuality and abortion are assumed by many members of the UN to be explicitly included in the existing UN treaties on human rights, but they are not. Despite this, in November 2017, the UN Human Rights Committee requested the Dominican Republic, a Catholic country, to legalise abortion in all cases where bringing the pregnancy to full term might cause *some damage* to the pregnant woman. Such a standard could, of course, be used to endorse virtually any abortion. In effect, it is an international demand on a sovereign nation to agree to the supposed right of every woman to abort her child at any stage.

The spreading religion of rights
Alongside the United Nations organisation, many activist groups around the world are strongly pursuing rights ideology.

In March 2015, Amnesty International presented a manifesto entitled *My Body My Rights*. Although the apparent purpose was to challenge hurtful discrimination and unnecessary criminalisation of vulnerable people, the start of the manifesto strongly declares that everyone has a human right to consensual sex with any other person, irrespective of anyone's sexuality, gender identity or marital status, and also a human right to unrestricted access to abortion.

How different this is from God's view of our bodies.

Do you not know that your body is a temple of the Holy Spirit who is in you, whom you have from God, and that you are not your own? For you have been bought with a price: therefore glorify God in your body. 1 Cor. 6:19-20

As a follower of Jesus, I consider my present body to be on a lifetime lease from my Maker. He has asked me to take care of it according to His instructions, to welcome Him there and to fulfil the earthly destiny that He has set before me. Thankfully, if it gets damaged by the storms of life or my bad choices, He is pleased to help with the repair of His property.

God must surely be very saddened to see such a libertarian manifesto, which will inevitably lead to spiritual, mental and physical disorder in the lives of countless individuals. Thank God that He is willing, at any time, to be given back the ownership of our bodies and, through Jesus Christ, to repair the damage that our hijacking of His property has caused.

In July 2016, an International AIDS Conference in Durban, South Africa, sponsored by UN agencies, intended as a further step in reducing and eradicating HIV/AIDS, was taken over by radical sexual rights activists. South Africa has the highest rates of HIV/AIDS infections in the world and government strategy promoting sexual rights has clearly failed. However, speaker after speaker at the conference blamed the high rates of infections on discrimination, sexism, racism and homophobia, while advocating new sexual freedoms such as the decriminalisation of the sex industry and the right of every child to experience sexual pleasure, however young. Incredibly, the very sexual behaviours that have driven the pandemic were justified and glorified in the name of sexual rights.

Sadly, there are countless examples of the relentless pressure on governments to conform to the latest rights ideology. In January 2018, a ruling was issued by the Inter-American Court of Human Rights ordering 16 countries to ignore their own national laws and recognise same-sex marriage and transgenderism. One commentator called the move 'the boldest exercise in judicial tyranny imaginable'. Human Rights Watch, a powerful and well-funded organisation based in New York, has recently been urging Barbados and other Eastern Caribbean nations to abandon their traditional cultures and promote same-sex marriage and liberal sexual education curricula in schools.

The grip of universal rights in Britain

In England, Scotland and Wales, The Equality and Human Rights Commission (EHRC) has responsibility for the promotion and enforcement of equality and human rights. The Commission is, in turn, bound by the articles of The European Convention on Human Rights, to which the UK is a signatory, and is required to provide advice on relevant acts passed by the UK government, such as the Equality Act 2010.

Over the last few years frequent conflicts in British law have appeared in relation to the issues of people's rights. For example, the European Court of Human Rights instructed the British government that it was in breach of prisoners' rights to deny them the vote in local and national elections, an instruction which has been a matter of dispute ever since. Many people are questioning what is happening to the laws of Britain, so painstakingly established through years of custom, practice and dependence on traditional Christian values.

Following the Marriage (Same Sex Couples) Act 2013, the

Commission felt it necessary to explain the implications of the Act in regard to the provision of school education. Key points stated that:

> *No school, or individual teacher, is under a duty to support, promote or endorse marriage of same sex couples... (subject to the requirement to meet duties under equality and human rights law) nothing in the Act affects the rights of schools with a religious character to continue to teach about marriage according to their religious doctrines and ethos.*

Many schools and teachers would say that, despite these apparent concessions to individual conscience, the pressure to conform to the 'politically correct' view of same-sex marriage as a fundamental and beneficial right is becoming overwhelming. In May 2018, the Office of Standards in Education was asked to consider new guidelines from the government (initially affecting independent schools) that would result in a school failing inspection if any teacher voices support for repeal of the Same-Sex Marriage Act. For countless Christians in Britain, it was the redefining of marriage, as being inclusive of those of the same sex, that has been one of the most significant acts of governmental undermining of our Christian heritage to date. It was, many argue, a decision in pursuance of equality rights that has put into question every boundary of reasonable constraint to sexual expression, sexual relationships and family life.

In pursuance of ever-increasing sexual rights, Christian doctors and nurses are under pressure to participate in gender reassignment of patients; Christian schools are under pressure to celebrate sexual licentiousness; Christian parents are under pressure to embrace their child's desire to pursue a change in gender identity; Christian politicians are under pressure to walk in gay-pride parades; Christian students are under pressure to sit through LBGTQ seminars, to avoid causing offence and being accused of discrimination.

Apparently recognising some of these pressures, an EHRC report from December 2016 commented, "There is no right in Britain not to be offended." In response to the report, the Deputy Director for Public Affairs at The Christian Institute wrote:

> *Christians have certainly felt that their fundamental freedoms have been set aside by the human rights and equality industry in recent years. We have long argued that equality law needs rebalancing so that courts have to take the time to weigh up competing rights to see if both sides can be reasonably accommodated. Too often the courts come down strongly in favour of the secular liberal side of the argument.*

These comments just sum up the dysfunction of where we have come to in Britain through allowing the religion of rights to become a primary determinate of justice in our society. No longer is any behaviour to be simply regarded as right or wrong. We are now left with the unsatisfactory situation of desperately trying to balance competing rights. The outcome is that *might* rather than *right* will often be the dominant factor in winning the argument, as the writer Thomas Carlyle perceptively stated many years ago in his book about the consequences of the French Revolution and the Declaration of the Rights of Man.

In summary

In 1948, reflecting the declarations concerning the rights of man written nearly two centuries before, the United Nations

General Assembly, meeting in Paris, ratified a strategic document referred to as The Universal Declaration of Human Rights. Faith in the ideology of the innate rights of man, to answer the needs of justice in the world, was given international status.

If this new faith in human rights was truly going to save the world, it needed to be systematically enforced upon every nation. Whilst the intentions may well have been good, the efficacy of universal human rights has remained doubtful at the least, and a gross deception at the worst. Under the umbrella of the United Nations, many nations have seen fit to adopt conventions and covenants in line with the 1948 declaration, thus strongly promoting the values of secular humanism in preference to any regard for traditional biblical views. The result has been that, although the concept of inalienable human rights has given considerable voice to many minority groups, some of whom have indeed been victims of serious oppression, the pursuance of this new religion has not given them any true solution. Instead, the consequence in society has frequently been more conflict that compassion.

In an October 2015 lecture to the Heritage Foundation in America, entitled *The Future of European Civilisation: Lessons for America*, the philosopher Sir Roger Scruton said:

> *During the 19th century, many Europeans thought they could compensate for the decline of the Christian faith by attaching themselves to ideologies [such as] nationalism, communism and Marxism. The rights panacea is the latest of these, but we know, or we ought to know, it does not work.*

Chapter 6

Humanism:
the doorway to the religion of rights

The beginnings of humanism
Humanism is a philosophy, life-stance and movement which emphasises the intellectual ability of mankind. It is the pursuit of man's ability to reason out the mysteries of life, elevated at the extreme to a position that denies the need for God. Historically, it has often been a reaction to authoritarian, corrupt and ritualistic religious practice. I have mentioned that humanist thinking goes back to certain schools of Greek and Roman philosophers. In fact, some Christian commentators believe that humanism, by its very

nature, is a natural product of the Greek mind rather than the Hebrew mind.

Christian writers like Erasmus, in the fifteenth century, simply wanted a rational as well as a revelatory approach to their exploration of scripture, but during the Enlightenment period, philosophers such as David Hume began to take a much more secular approach to the concept of humanism. Hume was part of a Scottish movement, and he has been titled by some as the first British sceptic, exploring the notion that human virtue could be achieved without any need for God. His primary project was to develop a science of human nature, a science of man and morality stripped of religious dogma and based on observable fact, utilitarianism and reasoned argument.

A more recent defining of humanism

In 1933 in the USA, a group of thirty-four intellectuals drew up a Humanist Manifesto. Interestingly, this referred to humanism as a religious movement replacing previous religions, which had been based on supernatural revelation.

The preamble of this manifesto stated:

> *Today, man's larger understanding of the universe, his scientific achievements ... have created a situation which requires a new statement of ... religion*

This was followed by fifteen statements, from which the following quotes give a flavour of the thinking behind the document:

> *Religious humanists regard the universe as self-existing and not created. Humanism asserts that the nature of the universe depicted by modern science makes unacceptable any supernatural or cosmic guarantees of human values. The goal of humanism is a free and universal society in which people voluntarily and intelligently cooperate for the common good ...*
>
> *... we consider the religious forms and ideas of our fathers no longer adequate ... Man is at last becoming aware that he alone is responsible for the realization of the world of his dreams, that he has within himself the power for its achievement.*

Further humanist statements followed over the next few decades which continued to deny the need for any supernatural input to the goal of improving man's condition. In a 1973 manifesto, for example, there was the line, "No deity will save us; we must save ourselves." Fundamental human rights also started to become a much stronger part of the ideology expressed in many of these documents, including, for example, a woman's right to abortion.

In 2002, a statement of the fundamental principles of modern humanism was passed unanimously by the General Assembly of the International Humanist and Ethical Union (IHEU) at the 50th anniversary of the World Humanist Congress in Amsterdam. According to the IHEU, the following declaration is the official definition of world humanism (bold added):

> *Humanism is a democratic and ethical life stance, which affirms that human beings have the* **right** *and responsibility to give meaning and shape to their own lives. It stands for the building of a more humane society through an ethic based on human and other natural values in the spirit of reason and free inquiry through human capabilities. It is not theistic and does not accept supernatural views of reality.*

The humanist agenda promoted by the IHEU can be summarised as follows:

* Promote humanism as non-theistic life stance throughout the world.
* Represent humanists within the international community.
* Defend human rights and the rights of humanists.
* Develop organised humanism in every part of the world.
* Build a strong and effective global organisation.

As with many movements that have promoted strongly-held political ideologies, humanists use well-established and frequently successful steps to advance their beliefs in society:

1. Promote tolerance of humanist ideology.
2. Promote equality of humanist ideology with other beliefs, in particular Christianity.
3. Promote reversal of traditional/Christian norms.
4. Promote legal action to establish humanist ideology.

It could well be argued that we have reached stage 4.

The Old Testament prophet Daniel found himself in a lion's den because of his refusal to bow to pressure, contrived by opponents, to obey a law that was in complete contradiction to his walk with God. Christians are increasingly facing similar challenges today from the activists of secular humanism. From a demand for a Christian baker to make a cake promoting gay marriage to a requirement for a Christian prison chaplain to refrain from preaching on challenging passages from the Bible, the law is being used to promote humanist ideology in stark opposition to authentic Christianity.

> *Then these men said, "We will not find any ground of accusation against this Daniel unless we find it against him with regard to the law of his God." Daniel 6:5*

It is dangerous to reason without God

Unless humans have an external arbiter of morality, the definition of an acceptable ethical life-stance is a negotiable issue, ever changing with politics and fashion. It becomes the pursuit of pleasure rather than righteousness. It depends on the fickle will of the people and not the steadfast will of God. I'm sure that those attending the World Humanist Congress in 2002 were mostly well-meaning, intelligent and considerate individuals, but there can be no doubt that their statement on humanism categorically opposed the beliefs of a follower of Jesus.

In contrast to this official statement of world humanism, we believe that it is God, rather than man, who gives meaning and shape to our lives. We believe that a humane society would exist if the laws and commands of God were obeyed, rather than trusting simply in the endeavours and capabilities of man. We believe in the existence of a Triune God: Father, Son and Holy Spirit. We believe that He works supernaturally in the lives of those who have accepted Jesus as Saviour and Lord of their lives. We believe Jesus to be the Way, the Truth and the Life.

Human rights are inextricably linked to humanism because

they both advocate the ultimate sovereignty of the individual rather than God. The right to determine the meaning and shape of our lives is taken from God and claimed by man. The assumption is that we are able not just to think for ourselves, but now we can reason out the mysteries of life without divine intervention; we are self-sufficient. Modern humanism is unashamedly secular, pursuing virtue through human reasoning alone. God has given human beings an extraordinary gift in being able to explore and reason out the physical laws of this world, but when it comes to spiritual issues, God gives us some critical advice, through His dialogue with the prophet Isaiah.

"Come now, let us reason together," says the LORD, "Though your sins are as scarlet, they will be as white as snow; though they are as red like crimson, they will be like wool. If you consent and obey, you will eat the best of the land; but if you refuse and rebel, you will be devoured by the sword." Truly, the mouth of the LORD has spoken. Isaiah 1:18–20

The language of secular humanism

The pressure and conflicts of humanism in the world today seem to strengthen on a daily basis. The most common cry is for freedom to live as each person believes is right for them, unrestrained by any imposed plumb-line of morality. The Bible has clear warnings in regard to this type of freedom:

Live as free people; do not, however, use your freedom to cover up any evil, but live as God's slaves. 1 Peter 2:16 (GNT)

As for you, my friends, you were called to be free. But do not let this freedom become an excuse for letting your physical desires control you. Instead, let love make you serve one another. Galatians 5:13 (GNT)

Humanism frequently returns to the much-stated idea that I should be able to enjoy unlimited freedom and rights, provided that I do others no harm. But this completely ignores the question of who decides what is harmful. As an example, albeit a somewhat bizarre one, there is a man in the UK, known as the naked rambler, who believes that he should have the right to walk wherever he chooses without wearing clothes. He is frequently in prison because, whenever he is released, he goes walking again and does so naked. He is adamant that his personal liberty and rights are being grossly infringed. The problem is that most people, particularly those with young children, would find it extremely offensive if the naked rambler were permitted to wander at will. If he were allowed this right, others might be forced to stay at home. When one man claims his desired freedom it commonly leads to another experiencing an undesired constraint.

Utilitarianism, another humanist term that came out of the Enlightenment, refers to the idea that all behaviour should be assessed on the basis of whether it would lead to more personal, or preferably more corporate, well-being or happiness. The activity from which the greatest number of people benefit is regarded, in this philosophy, as having the greatest value. It is a theoretical concept of morality that is totally unworkable, for, at the extreme, it would justify the death of any particular individual disliked by his peers!

The United States Declaration of Independence picked up this pursuit of happiness for every human being by naming it as a God-given right. Not only is this untrue but it is also unwise; happiness does not come from the pursuit of pleasure, nor is it guaranteed by freedom. Many wealthy people experiencing almost unlimited freedom of action have spiralled into depression and sometimes suicide. True happiness, or rather joy, actually comes from renunciation of rights; this is the challenge of the Christian message.

The demand for equality is also a central theme for rights activists, but it's a word that is meaningless without a moral framework to give it definition. It is worth repeating that, for followers of Jesus, equality means giving the same value to every human being, irrespective of background, belief or behaviour. It does not mean saying that every belief, behaviour or lifestyle is equally acceptable to God.

Humanists do not accept the existence of moral absolutes and certainly not religious values. So, views of ethical behaviour are ever-changing, fed by a multitude of politicised ideas, using key words such as freedom, equality, inclusivity, diversity and of course rights.

Questioning the validity of these ideologies now increasingly results in the use of other key words such as intolerance, discrimination, bigotry, prejudice and narrow-mindedness.

The dominant issues particularly being used to challenge traditional Christian beliefs today are marriage, abortion, sexual attraction and transgenderism. Inclusivity is a key concept for many rights activists; all lifestyles are to be accepted and welcomed as a fundamental human right. The United Nations organisation, along with the European Union and the governments of certain key countries such as Canada, at the time of writing, seem to be taking a leading role as self-proclaimed arbiters of international morality. The latest opinion of a UN committee now carries far more weight, internationally, than

the unchanging plumb-line of God's Word. To disagree with these opinions is seen as unlawful discrimination against those in society who are automatically deemed to be victims of outdated prejudice.

I was interested to see the following news headline recently which, incidentally, made no mention of violence towards unborn children:

> *The UN Committee on the Elimination of Discrimination against Women (CEDAW) has drawn up a report in which it accuses the UK of 'violence against women' because of Northern Ireland's pro-life laws.*

Jesus was the most inclusive person ever to walk the earth, in His acceptance of every sinner, but He strongly discriminated against human sin, for He knew the damage this was causing in people's lives.

Humanism is dependent on the promotion of universal human rights

"I have an innate right to shape my own life," says the humanist. Many political leaders (who seem increasingly led by social trending rather than personal principles) say, "That sounds very reasonable to us." Consequently, we live in a world where people are being increasingly encouraged to actively claim their rights without, very often, having any understanding of the validity or consequence of such rights. The overall message is that there are undeniable entitlements concerning lifestyle and behaviour which we are foolish not to pursue. A few might say that rights should surely go hand in hand with responsibilities, but the dominant voice says, "You have rights, not least in your lifestyle choice, and you should make sure that you enjoy as much licence as everyone else, and you must fight any discrimination against your exercising of those rights."

Is it surprising that we are living in an increasingly selfish and contentious world? Is this not the inevitable consequence of the promotion of a humanistic lifestyle based on the claiming of rights rather than consideration of what is truly right or wrong? Amazingly, shortly after writing this last sentence, I heard a commentator on the radio say exactly these words: "There is no concept of goodness or badness in people's decisions of lifestyle today."

Let's take a moment to reflect more deeply on two examples of particular lifestyle choices which are being given validity through the ideologies of equality and rights. Of course, the world is free to adopt these choices, but we need to be very clear about where the Bible stands on these issues.

I have a right to end my life when I choose. Assisted dying in situations of significant personal distress is seen as an acceptable solution by many in the world, but it is not God's way. He alone should determine the appointed time of someone's death (Ecclesiastes 3:1–2). As followers of Jesus Christ, and a part of God's family, we can be confident that the enemy need retain no power over our death or the fear of death.

> *...that through death He [Jesus] might render powerless him who had the power of death, that is, the devil, and might free those who through fear of death were subject to slavery all their lives.* Hebrews 2:14b–15

I have a right to marry someone of the same sex. Many regard this step as simply offering equality of opportunity, but the use of the word *marriage* for a same-sex union is both a contradiction of biblical truth and a misleading statement of equality. The intimate consummation of a same-sex couple can never be equal to that of a man and woman, nor can a same-sex union ever lead to the natural procreation of children. In the name of equality, the incorporating of homosexual and lesbian partnerships into the meaning of the word marriage is a dramatic departure from God's order (Matthew 19:5). The right of some to now use this word for same-sex union will forever conflict with the right of others to use the word to mean only what it has meant for countless generations.

As with so many of these issues founded on rights, it seems to come down to having to agree with those who have the power rather than the legitimacy, similar to the inevitable surrender that we would give to the aircraft hijacker holding a gun. Today, the expression of traditional Christian faith is facing frequent and powerful legal challenges never considered possible a few years ago. Rights-based justice will regularly end in competing positions about who can claim to be the real victim in the case, rather than finding a truly righteous resolution.

Should a Christian nurse with strong beliefs about the Bible's view of gender have the right to decline participation in the process of attaching synthetic genitals to a woman who chooses to change her appearance to look like a man? Or does the belief and right of the transgender person take precedence? In the distressing issue of gender dysphoria, the Christian is likely to genuinely believe that it is the heart of the person that needs reshaping by God, whereas the humanist is more likely to believe it is the body that must be reshaped by a medical team. The answer is surely not to enforce rights but to allow freedom of belief and counsel.

The spearhead of sexual rights

We live in a world where countless people are struggling with sexual brokenness, a wounded sexual identity often caused by an abusive childhood. The need for inner healing has never been more necessary. However, the dominant voice, in the face of so much sexual dysfunction, is not a call for the repair of broken lives but for the pursuit of sexual rights.

According to activists, sexual rights cover the promotion of individual freedom in areas of contraception, abortion, sexual expression (including cross-dressing and nudity), pornography, age of consent, sexual orientation, gender identity, hormone therapy, sex-change operations, adultery, sodomy, prostitution, adoption, fertility services and sexuality education.

The rights agenda concerning sexuality is being particularly targeted at children, irrespective of parental views. In January 2018, the United Nations Educational, Scientific and Cultural Organisation (UNESCO) updated its Comprehensive Sexuality Education policy to include instruction to children as young as five years old about their own gender, body rights, genitals and sexual contact. According to the policy, children as young as nine should be instructed on the meaning of rape and pornography, and told that their gender identity might not match their biological sex.

As of 2018 the Scottish government is proposing changes in the law regarding gender recognition. These proposals include allowing children to legally change their gender at 16 or 17 years of age, and allowing children of any age to seek to change gender without parental consent by appealing to the courts. In reality, the thousands of genetic differences between men and women cannot be changed by hormones or surgery; only a change in gender appearance is possible. In the name of sexual rights, children are being encouraged to live a lie.

Activists are not truly fighting discrimination in regard to issues of sexual equality but are fighting a legal battle against the Bible's position on sexual morality. This plumb-line has served as a civilising constraint on humanity from the time of God's covenant with His chosen race, the Jews, when He separated them from the licentious behaviour of a pagan world.

Our failure in the Body of Christ to make known His truths

In contrast to the true life-giving message of the Word of God, the Church, over many centuries, has all too often delivered a condemning and inauthentic answer to the needs of those struggling with oppressed and broken lives. It's not surprising that many have sought a humanistic alternative to so much irrelevant religious practice.

The supernatural nature of God has been discredited by spiritual excesses, false miracles or, more usually, widespread unbelief. But there *is* a God of miracles. He *does* supernaturally restore broken and bound lives. He *does* give us laws and commands by which to live at peace. He *does* shape the character of those who are surrendered to the One who walked this earth in complete obedience to His Father. He *does* give us the right to be called His children, if we acknowledge our sinfulness and receive His forgiveness. These truths need to be confidently and graciously presented to a world experiencing so much spiritual famine. Secular humanism will never meet the deep hunger of humankind for order and justice. We need to graciously but clearly state that God's means of bringing justice and healing is based entirely upon the resolution of sin, and this cannot be circumvented through the false religions of humanism and human rights.

Interestingly, in February 2018, six Republican House members in the United States filed the Marriage and Constitution Act, which argued that same-sex marriage is part of "the religion of Secular Humanism" and, as such, its imposition is unconstitutional. The Body of Christ needs to be bold in holding up a plumb-line of biblical truth which, at the very least, makes clear to the world where the laws of a nation are deviating from the laws of God.

Sin and the sinful nature

Secular humanists dismiss the concept of sin and yet they often take an aggressive stance against anyone who challenges their particular ethical code of rights. The issue is that their code has the attraction, for them, of being able to be renegotiated at any time, and so make allowance for changing attitudes, whereas

God's definition of sin is unchanging. The enemy would be delighted if humans completely disregarded the biblical concepts of good, evil, righteousness and the sinful nature. He would be very happy indeed to see them replaced with the less offensive idea of universal rights, and for this to be promoted through an aggressive condemnation of any discrimination against those rights.

In Britain, the traditional biblical concepts of right and wrong are disappearing very quickly under a confusing and destructive tsunami of claimed entitlements. An English judge, Lord Denning, spoke the following words during an address to the Lawyers' Prayer Union back in 1952:

> *It is, I suggest to you, a most significant thing that a judge should draw... his principles of justice from the Christian commandment of love. I do not know where else he is to find them... The common law of England has been moulded for centuries by judges who have been brought up in the Christian faith. The precepts of religion, consciously or unconsciously, have been their guide in the administration of justice.*

Compare this with the following words spoken by High Court judge Sir James Munby in an October 2013 lecture to the Law Society in London, entitled *The Sacred and the Secular*:

> *Religion is no longer the business of judges... The courts should not try to be guardians of morality because there is no longer one definition of right and wrong in the wake of the sexual revolution... Judges should now take people as*

> *they find them... Beliefs about matters such as sex outside marriage or homosexuality held by the majority in the early 1960s are as distant to modern Britons as ancient civilisations such as Nineveh or Babylon.*

However, let's take a moment to remind ourselves of what God says about these issues of right and wrong. He is neither confused, nor is He going to ever change His views. Goodness is not about being a nice person but rather giving a reflection of the perfect nature and character of God.

"Why do you ask me concerning what is good?" answered Jesus. "There is only One who is good. Keep the commandments if you want to enter life." Matthew 19:17 (GNT)

Evil is not just about being bad. It is instead a reflection of the rebellious nature and character of Satan. It pervades every part of the world in which we live.

We know that we belong to God even though the whole world is under the rule of the Evil One. 1 John 5:19 (GNT)

Righteousness is not about religious behaviour but a heart condition of being right with God's laws and commands, through confession of sin.

If we confess our sins, He is faithful and righteous to forgive us our sins and to cleanse us from all unrighteousness. 1 John 1:9

The sinful nature describes the uncomfortable biblical fact that every human being is born not with a God-given right to life, but with an inbuilt tendency to sin, resulting from the Fall.

It is a condition that actually deserves death. Before the Fall, human beings had the *potential* for sin; after the Fall they had the *taste* for it! Paul was only too aware of the battle that raged within him, even as a believer in Jesus.

> *For I know that good itself does not dwell in me, that is, in my sinful nature. For I have the desire to do what is good, but I cannot carry it out. Romans 7:18 (NIV)*

Sadly, the sinful nature does not want to submit to divine rule through the human spirit but to promote dominance of the human soul. This rule of the soul over the spirit has been the default setting of sinful man ever since the Fall. The Bible refers to it as natural or soulish (*Greek: psuchikos*) behaviour.

> *But the natural [psuchikos] man does not accept the things of the Spirit of God, for they are foolishness to him; and he cannot understand them, because they are spiritually appraised. But he who is spiritual [pneumatikos] appraises all things, yet he himself is appraised by no one. 1 Corinthians 2:14–15*

When our human soul claims entitlement that has not been given by God, we are assuming personal sovereignty, and this soulish lifestyle not only lacks divine wisdom but also gives rights to the enemy.

> *...don't sin against the truth by boasting of your wisdom. Such wisdom does not come down from heaven; it belongs to the world, it is unspiritual [psuchikos] and demonic. James 3:14b–15 (GNT)*

Humanism refuses to look at the condition of man from God's point of view, preferring to believe in man's ability to achieve virtue by his own reason, wisdom and effort. To ignore the biblical certainty of man's sin and to rely solely on the notion of man's rights is to play into the enemy's deceptive hands. It is New Age belief that spiritual restoration of humans is possible through countless alternative therapies and techniques, from bioenergy healing to crystal therapy, but not one of these remedies recognises the need for God's forgiveness of sin, the only means by which we can receive His true healing.

If we say that we have no sin, we deceive ourselves, and there is no truth in us. 1 John 1:8 (GNT)

Personal sovereignty – the foundational demand of humanism

The LORD has established His throne in the heavens, and His sovereignty rules over all. Psalm 103:19

Contention between God and humankind over the issue of spiritual sovereignty goes back to the Fall. I have defined sovereignty as the position of authority which requires no accountability. From a biblical perspective, this position can only be held by the God of creation. It is only logical that the Creator of human life must be the One to whom we are accountable, but the fallen nature of man is such that we would much rather hold that place of sovereignty ourselves.

Man has tried at least three solutions to overcome this carnal conflict between his authority and the authority of God. The first solution, which we see at the Fall, is to rebel against God, ignore His instructions, act as if man is sovereign and hope that the consequence will not be too severe.

Another solution, which was evident, for example, at the time of the French Revolution, was to adopt the view that there probably is a distant Supreme Being but, having somehow set the universe in motion, he, or perhaps it, cares little for our daily wellbeing. Such a deity certainly would not require us to be directly accountable to divine instruction, and so, we conclude, our claiming of human sovereignty and rights is unlikely to cause much divine upset.

A third solution has been to adopt the ideology of the secular humanist and declare that there is no God, our existence is entirely the consequence of chance, and humans are therefore fully entitled to hold the place of sovereignty in the known universe, by virtue of their unsurpassable intelligence.

Jesus came to deal with all of man's sin, not least his pride, and to make it clear to us that all authority has been given to Him. He gives mankind the opportunity to abandon his foolish assumptions of sovereignty and to surrender to the King of kings. He loves us too much to leave us so confused and so spiritually vulnerable. The Bible clearly tells us that all authority in heaven and on earth originates in God, and He releases whatever authority is necessary on earth for the ordering of nations, families and individuals.

Christ rules there above all heavenly rulers, authorities, powers, and lords; he has a title superior to all titles of authority in this world and in the next. Ephesians 1:21 (GNT)

"By Me kings reign, and rulers decree justice." Proverbs 8:15

When the people of a nation ignore these biblical truths in favour of people-power, divine order is lost and there will always be consequences. The result can be, at worst, gross disorder such as we saw so clearly in the Reign of Terror following the French Revolution.

In summary
Although many people are, no doubt, sincere in their belief in

the benefits of secular humanism, the agenda of the movement, at least in Western culture, is complete removal from society of all the norms of Judeo-Christian belief and tradition. According to the Bible this is serious error.

Woe to those who call evil good, and good evil; who substitute darkness for light and light for darkness; who substitute bitter for sweet and sweet for bitter! Woe to those who are wise in their own eyes and clever in their own sight! Isaiah 5:20–21

A significant aspect of the ideology of humanism is the concept of human beings having the ultimate right to determine the shape and meaning of their own lives. Universal human rights will always be a focus of secular humanism because together they are able to fully express the necessary denial of the sovereignty of God while giving prominence to the sovereignty of the individual.

Chapter 7

Rights, Contracts and Covenants

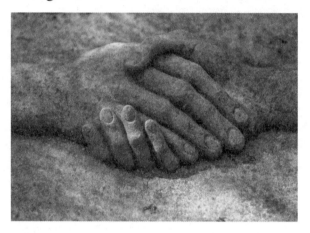

Covenants are serious

The distribution of rights is an integral part of any agreement between two or more parties. They define matters of licence, commitment, payment and entitlement, for example, confirming the benefits to be obtained by those making the agreement. In the business world such agreements, or contracts, involve an exchange of goods or services, with agreed terms and conditions. A covenant, however, is a much more serious agreement because it implies a deep commitment of lives. Frequently in the Bible, a covenant was literally a matter of life and death, not least in the case of God's covenant with His chosen people the Jews, a covenant He later extended to all mankind, for those willing to accept the terms.

From the time of the 1948 Universal Declaration many

further documents have sought to strengthen the observance of human rights as the primary basis of international justice. There have been agreements and charters such as The International Covenant on Economic, Social and Cultural Rights (1966); The International Covenant on Civil and Political Rights (1976); and The Charter of Fundamental Rights of the European Union (2000).

The preamble of the International Covenant on Civil and Political Rights states that:

> *In accordance with the principles proclaimed in the Charter of the United Nations ... the obligation of the States [the participating nations] under the Charter is to promote the universal respect for, and observance of, human rights and freedoms... recognized in the present Covenant.*

It is significant that the participating nations thought it wise to enshrine the ideology of rights within a covenantal framework, beyond the normal terms of political treaties. In describing themselves as covenanted together on the issue of human rights, whether they realised it or not, the signatories were declaring a spiritual binding of these nations to this humanistic ideology. This surely plays right into the hands of the spiritual ruler of this world, as man-made covenants can seriously conflict with the covenant that God desires with humanity.

Sir Roger Scruton wrote in a June 2014 article entitled *The Good of Government*:

> *Everywhere in the European Union, a regime of political correctness makes it difficult either to maintain, or to live by, precepts that violate the state-imposed orthodoxies. Non-discrimination laws force many religious people to go against the teachings of their faith.*

Who presides over these recent covenant agreements?

Unlike the United States Declaration of Independence and the French Declaration of the Rights of Man in the eighteenth century, a higher spiritual authority is not mentioned in any of the international documents on rights from 1948 onward. This, of course, allows the content to be inclusive of all religious persuasions, but it leaves open the question as to what spiritual authority is overseeing this binding together of nations in proclaiming innate human rights.

For certain nations wishing to incorporate international declarations into their own national constitutions, the absence of divine justification and oversight caused a problem, so God got reintroduced! The preamble to the Canadian Bill of Rights of 1960 echoes the American declaration of 1776:

> *The Canadian Nation is founded upon the principles that acknowledge the supremacy of God, the dignity and worth of the human person and the position of the family in a society of free men and free institutions... also that men and institutions remain free only when freedom is founded upon respect for moral and spiritual values and the rule of law; and [is] desirous of enshrining these principles and the human rights and fundamental freedoms derived from them.*

I noticed in the summer 2017 issue of *Jubilee* an article by Canadian lawyer Andre Schutten, entitled *Liberty and Freedom in Canada at 150*, which included this important statement in regard to the Canadian Bill of Rights:

> *We can possess a genuine right only if it comes from Someone who has the authority to grant it.*

The problem with the very laudable wording of the preamble to the Canadian Bill of Rights is that it states that the principle of fundamental human rights for every Canadian citizen is derived from acknowledgement of the supremacy of God; but, once again, this derivation is ill-founded. As Andre Schutten says, the declaration of human rights is indeed unsupportable without the higher "Someone", but it's also unsupportable because the only "Someone" who has the true authority to confer such universal rights did not in fact do it! The enemy, I suggest, is only too pleased to be given the opportunity to hijack this authority for himself.

The divine "Someone" grants rights only through obedience

However good the intention of these declarations might be, universal human rights outside of a covenant with God are simply a man-made idea. Even the seemingly obvious concept of the *right to life* is challenged by the fact that God looks at the issue of life and death in a completely different way. He does not say that fallen man will find personal security by claiming an innate right to life, but He does say very clearly to us all, "Do not murder." In fact, Jesus expressed God's views concerning human life more strongly, by saying that even bad-mouthing someone else is tantamount to murder in His justice system.

"You have heard that people were told in the past, 'Do not commit murder; anyone who does will be brought to trial.' But now I tell you: if you are angry with your brother you will be brought to trial, if you call your brother 'You good-for-nothing!' you will be brought before the Council, and if you call your brother a worthless fool you will be in danger of going to the fire of hell." Matthew 5:21–22 (GNT)

May I take the opportunity to say this yet again: in God's Kingdom, His blueprint for all justice is based on recognising and dealing with sin, not on claiming rights. He put before His chosen people, the Jews, the option of being obedient to Him and finding life, or being disobedient and knowing death (Deuteronomy 30:15–20). It may not always seem fair to our human reasoning, but God has now made a way for us to be certain of finding abundant and eternal life. It is achieved through the Lordship of Jesus Christ. God's ways are not our ways and His measure of righteousness is far beyond what man can achieve without the intervention of a Saviour.

Understanding the biblical significance of covenant

Let's consider a little more deeply the biblical concept of covenant, and the associated rights. From the earliest times of the Bible, the idea of covenant was known even to those outside of God's chosen people and was a common aspect of life among the early patriarchs. Covenants were agreements made with specific vows, with oaths invoking divine authority, and often sealed by a ritual of sacrifice.

We'll take a moment to look at a particular example in the Bible, of an agreement that was not enacted in obedience to God and shows the deadly seriousness of a wrong covenant. It's the story of the Gibeonites. The inhabitants of Gibeon had heard about the victories of Joshua and they decided to avoid a fight by sending envoys who pretended to have come from well beyond the land that God had given to the Children of Israel. These envoys sought a treaty with Joshua, even making themselves and their luggage appear worn-out from a supposed long journey. They held out some of their food to show its stale condition, and the men of Israel were taken in.

> *So the men of Israel took some of their provisions, and did not ask for the counsel of the LORD. Joshua made peace with them and made a covenant with them, to let them live; and the leaders of the congregation swore an oath to them. Joshua 9:14–15*

In line with many biblical covenants, it was an agreement between a strong tribe and a weaker one, on this occasion securing a right for the Gibeonites to live in peace. Shortly afterwards, Joshua realised his mistake, but it was too late, for he knew that he had entered into an unbreakable covenant by making an oath before God, even though God had not instructed the treaty. So the men of Israel had to live with the Gibeonites occupying some of the Promised Land, a situation which was very likely to lead to problems.

Many generations later we learn that Saul had murdered some of the Gibeonites and, as a spiritual consequence to this breaking of covenant between God's people and the Gibeonites, severe famine had hit the land under the reign of King David.

> *During David's reign there was a severe famine which lasted for three full years. So David consulted the LORD about it, and the LORD said, "Saul and his family are guilty of murder; he put the people of Gibeon to death." 2 Samuel 21:1 (GNT)*

We are then told that it cost the lives of seven of Saul's descendants before the curse of this wrong covenant was broken and fruitfulness returned to the land. Interestingly, Jonathan's son Mephibosheth was only spared because of a previous covenant agreement between David and Jonathan. Covenants are indeed serious commitments from a biblical perspective, and we should not enter them lightly. They carry a powerful spiritual significance, holding those involved in a binding compact, such as that intended in godly marriage (Malachi 2:14).

I suggest that Joshua's ungodly covenant with the Gibeonites and the consequences it had on the people of future generations might well have echoes in the ungodly international covenants on human rights that are being entered into today: powerful agreements based on misguided faith in the universal and inalienable rights of man. Where God is not honoured by the rulers of this world, there will surely be trouble ahead! Covenants made by humankind outside of God's instructions can be very dangerous. The enemy understands the significance of covenant and will take any opportunity to gain an advantage through man's pursuing of wrongful agreements.

A more recent destructive covenant

In 1912, borrowing some of the beliefs and language of the Scottish Covenanters of the seventeenth century, the protestant community in Ireland covenanted together, supposedly under God, to oppose, by *all means that might be found necessary*, the British Home Rule Bill which they considered likely to result in a Catholic government in Dublin. Here is the wording of that covenant agreement (bold added):

> *BEING CONVINCED in our consciences that Home Rule would be disastrous to the material well-being of Ulster as well as of the whole of Ireland, subversive of our civil and religious freedom, destructive of our citizenship, and perilous to the unity of the Empire, we, whose names are underwritten, men of Ulster, loyal subjects of His Gracious Majesty King George V, humbly relying on the God whom our fathers in days of stress and trial confidently trusted,* **do hereby pledge ourselves in solemn Covenant,** *throughout this our time of threatened calamity, to stand by one another in defending, for ourselves and our children, our cherished position of equal citizenship in the United Kingdom, and in* **using all means which may be found necessary** *to defeat the present conspiracy to set up a Home Rule Parliament in Ireland. And in the event of such a Parliament being forced upon us, we further solemnly and mutually pledge ourselves to refuse to recognise its authority.* **In sure confidence that God will defend the right**, *we hereto subscribe our names.*

It is pertinent that this covenant was essentially declaring a God-ordained right to challenge the authority of the government of the day, even by use of arms, over an issue of supposed religious freedom. Many believe that this ungodly covenant was, at the very least, part of the spiritual doorway that has led to a century of bloodshed in Ireland. The concerns of the protestant community may well have been valid in some measure, but to enter into a rebellious covenant before God, claiming rights that were in violation of the Word of God, is not the way of His Kingdom.

Everyone must obey state authorities, because no authority exists without God's permission, and the existing authorities have been put there by God. Whoever opposes the existing authority opposes what God has ordered; and anyone who does so will bring judgment on himself. Romans 13:1–2 (GNT)

Of course, rulers and governments are imperfect and even, at times, downright wicked. It is right to strongly challenge sinful practice, but this verse from Romans tells us that all structures of authority originate from God, however much they have been contaminated by man's sin. God's way of restoring justice and righteousness is to expose and confront the sin of rulers and seek rightful justice, rather than to enter into a binding covenant declaring a right of armed rebellion.

The need for citizens' rights within a nation

I have acknowledged that justice within every nation does require some form of constitutional agreement between those ruled and those ruling, a *social contract*. Achieving this delicate relationship has been a primary issue behind the concept of rights throughout history. The problem of harsh rulers oppressing the citizens of a nation has frequently led to a very understandable call for legal freedoms and rights for the populace. We have seen that unjust rule led to the English Magna Carta and the French Declaration of the Rights of Man, and many other strategic documents seeking a fair relationship between all levels of society.

The intent of such a contract is that citizens within a nation consent to surrender some of their desired freedoms, and to submit to the authority of a ruler, or government, in exchange for protection of remaining rights. Such an agreement makes sense in seeking to establish a well-ordered society. However, these citizens' rights are not necessarily natural or innate human rights. They are simply privileges (which must go along with personal responsibilities) which are established within a statutory contract, in order to give reasonable freedom to the individual, sufficient authority to the government and security to the populace as a whole.

God endorses the just statutes within a nation and the recognition of these rights for every citizen, however poor, and He warns against governmental abuse:

> *Woe to those who enact evil statutes and to those who constantly record unjust decisions, so as to deprive the needy of justice and rob the poor of My people of their rights, so that widows may be their spoil and that they may plunder the orphans. Isaiah 10:1–2*

Paul successfully claimed his legal rights as a Roman citizen when he was being falsely accused and punished in Jerusalem.

> *But when they had tied him up to be whipped, Paul said to the officer standing there, "Is it lawful for you to whip a Roman citizen who hasn't even been tried for any crime?" Acts 22:25 (GNT)*

He used these citizen rights even to demand an audience with Caesar and was thus given the opportunity to defend his

faith in front of high-ranking politicians such as Felix, Festus and Agrippa. Paul was using his rights as a citizen of Rome, but he was not claiming them to be universal human rights.

Sometimes the courtroom can give an ideal opportunity to speak out the gospel message, and God can certainly choose to use man-made citizens' rights to further His purposes. Interestingly, in the nineteenth century, Wilberforce found it politically prudent to focus his arguments on establishing the legitimate rights of slaves rather than on the sin of the slave-owners, in trying to get his anti-slavery laws through the British parliament.

God's plan of Kingship and covenant with humankind

The Bible tells us that God has always intended a unique form of agreement in His relationship with human beings. He describes Himself as ruling over a Kingdom but He has made it clear that the entitlements within His Kingdom are to be conferred through a divine *covenant* with His people, not a divine *contract*. This covenant, although entirely relevant to Adam, was explained and established more specifically through Abraham and then through Moses for the Children of Israel. The key to this chosen people receiving the privileges of such an agreement was to be their obedience to God's instructions. The rights of this special relationship were only for those keeping to the terms of the divine covenant.

'Now then, if you will indeed obey My voice and keep My covenant, then you shall be My own possession among all the peoples, for all the earth is Mine; and you shall be to Me a kingdom of priests and a holy nation'. Exodus 19:5–6a

God's plan was that the detailed instructions of His rule as King would be discerned by chosen individuals, called judges in the Bible, and these men or women would give the King's direction to the people. Unfortunately, after a while, His people did not want God as King, but rather sought an earthly king in line with other nations. Samuel, in his old age, took the brunt of their grumblings, and God advised him as to what he should say and do.

...and the LORD said, "Listen to everything the people say to you. You are not the one they have rejected; I am the one they have rejected as their king. Ever since I brought them out of Egypt, they have turned away from me and worshiped other gods; and now they are doing to you what they have always done to me. So then, listen to them, but give them strict warnings and explain how their kings will treat them."
1 Samuel 8:7–9 (GNT)

So, the Children of Israel got their kings and often paid a heavy price through the sinfulness of these rulers, just as God had warned. The people had been told that kings would be far more self-centred than God-centred. King David was among the few who seemed to really understand the true nature of God's ultimate Kingship over His people.

The LORD placed his throne in heaven; he is king over all.
Psalm 103:19 (GNT)

A specific right of the Jewish people to possession of land

One of the stated entitlements of the covenant between God and the descendants of Abraham was the divine promise of permanent ownership of a designated area of land, referred to as the whole land of Canaan. This conferred right, explained by God to Abraham, was a consequence of God's decision to set apart a particular people, and was dependent upon their willingness to be marked out by the particular sign of male circumcision.

"The whole land of Canaan will belong to your descendants forever, and I will be their God." God said to Abraham, "You also must agree to keep the covenant with me, both you and your descendants in future generations. You and your

descendants must all agree to circumcise every male among you." Genesis 17:8b–10 (GNT)

It is interesting to reflect on mankind's loss of the right to rule over the earth at the Fall, a right handed over to Satan as a result of man following the enemy's instructions rather than those of God. It seems that God has always intended for us to know His delegation of spiritual and practical authority over the land, in order to reflect the full meaning of His character of fruitfulness. It is not surprising therefore that, in setting apart a nation to demonstrate His desired covenant relationship with humankind, He included the promise of dominion over a designated land.

He has remembered His covenant forever, the word which He commanded to a thousand generations, the covenant which He made with Abraham, and His oath to Isaac. Then He confirmed it to Jacob for a statute, to Israel as an everlasting covenant, saying, "To you I will give the land of Canaan as the portion of your inheritance." Psalm 105:8–11

Amazingly, we have been able to see the ongoing fulfilment of that covenant right of the Jewish people in the last 120 years of the history of the Holy Land. In 1897, at the summons of a visionary individual called Theodore Herzl, the First Zionist Congress was convened in order to promote a legal right for the Jewish people to have a national homeland in the land of Israel. This movement towards reinstatement of a Jewish state was further strengthened by the famous Balfour Declaration of 1917, a letter written on behalf of the United Kingdom government by the then foreign secretary:

> *His Majesty's government view with favour the*
> *establishment in Palestine of a national home for the*
> *Jewish people, and will use their best endeavours to*
> *facilitate the achievement of this object...*

In 1922, following the end of the First World War and the overthrow of the Ottoman Empire, the League of Nations gave unanimous international legitimacy to this right in the Palestine Mandate, which declared:

> *Recognition has been given to the historical connection*
> *of the Jewish people with Palestine and to the grounds for*
> *reconstituting their national home in that country.*

In an extraordinary way, the world-governing authorities of the time were endorsing the ancient and irrevocable covenant promises of God to the Jewish people. Despite considerable failures by the British government in their trusteeship of Palestine over the following thirty years, and the military opposition from the surrounding Arab states, on 14ᵗʰ May 1948 in a little art museum on Rothschild Boulevard in Tel Aviv, David Ben-Gurion, leader

of the Jewish National Council, announced the formation of the state of Israel. The first independent Jewish state in nineteen centuries of history was formed by his reading out the following proclamation (bold added):

> *By virtue of the natural and* **historic right** *of the Jewish people and by resolution of the General Assembly of the United Nations, we hereby proclaim the establishment of a Jewish state in Palestine to be called Israel.*

Actually, this was not so much a *natural* right of the Jewish people but a *divinely conferred* right, given by God in a covenant agreement with Abraham. This was a truly inalienable right to ownership of land, conferred on a specific people group. Interestingly, an international human rights lawyer from Toronto, Jacques Gauthier, who spent 25 years conducting research into conflicting claims to Jerusalem under international law, stated the following in an address to the European Parliament in Brussels, on Jerusalem Day, May 2011 (bold added):

> *The Jewish people are in Jerusalem, not as settlers or invaders, but* **as of right.** *These rights are clearly spelt out in international law and should be respected by the international community. For anyone who is interested in justice, these are issues which we have to study very carefully.* **The rights vested in the Jewish people stand on very solid legal ground and are valid to this day.** *Jerusalem is not a settlement but the historical capital of Israel. If Jerusalem were to be divided along the armistice demarcation lines of 1967, it would place the Old City under Palestinian rule. This would contradict the legal commitments made to the Jewish people in the San Remo Resolution of 1920, the Mandate for Palestine in 1922, as well as Article 80 in the United Nations Charter.*

How amazing that the God-given rights to land which He conferred on the Jewish people through Abraham, some four thousand years ago, would be given endorsement in international law over these last hundred years.

The coming of the King:
A new covenant extended to the whole of mankind

God spoke through the prophets of the Old Testament about His plan to establish a new covenantal relationship with human beings through One who was to come and reign forever. Furthermore, this new opportunity of citizenship in His Kingdom would be for the whole of mankind, if they chose to accept the King's rule. This was to be a new divine covenant bringing true human rights and true justice to mankind.

> *A child is born to us! A son is given to us! And he will be our ruler. He will be called, "Wonderful Counsellor," "Mighty God," "Eternal Father," "Prince of Peace." His royal power will continue to grow; his kingdom will always be at peace. He will rule as King David's successor, basing his power on right and justice, from now until the end of time. The LORD Almighty is determined to do all this. Isaiah 9:6–7 (GNT)*

Of course, it was Jesus, the Son of God, who came and restored the reality of a divine Kingdom, enabling it to operate on earth today through His followers walking as citizens of that Kingdom. This was to be in the midst of a world that seems, sadly, determined to seek a just society more through human wisdom than the wisdom of the Creator. The Bible constantly challenges this arrogance of man.

> *Never let yourself think that you are wiser than you are; simply obey the LORD and refuse to do wrong. Proverbs 3:7 (GNT)*

God explained His Kingdom principles of justice firstly through the Torah, the written laws of the Old Covenant, then through the words of Jesus in a New Covenant. These stand as the model of how God sees the rightful ordering of society, but most people in the world reject this model, and He will never coerce them into obedience. The commands of God are clear in the Bible but He has given man a freewill choice to obey Him or disobey Him. Followers of Jesus can and should declare what they believe to be right, but we cannot expect a world governed by secular humanism and false religions to be eager to walk according to biblical truth. The Body of Christ just needs to be careful not to be led off the right pathway by well-meaning arguments or aggressive accusations of discrimination against the supposed rights of others.

What does God say is right in His Kingdom?

The ways of God's Kingdom are radically different from the world. Even as believers, however much we might think our assessment of a situation is fair and just, Jesus explains that God usually thinks very differently! In Matthew chapter 5, particularly, Jesus gives the true intent and spirit of the written laws of the Old Covenant. These Mosaic laws and commands of His Kingdom had been right for His chosen people, and Jesus makes it clear that the essence of these laws would never be abolished. However, under God's new covenant with His people, being reconciled to God and knowing the rights of citizenship in His Kingdom would require a complete change of thinking, well beyond just the following of written rules.

So then, whoever disobeys even the least important of the commandments and teaches others to do the same, will be least in the Kingdom of heaven. On the other hand, whoever obeys the Law and teaches others to do the same, will be great in the Kingdom of heaven. I tell you, then, that you will be able to enter the Kingdom of heaven only if you are more faithful than the teachers of the Law and the Pharisees in doing what God requires. Matthew 5:19–20 (GNT)

Jesus continues His challenge by showing the disciples the difference between their thinking and God's thinking with respect to justice and rights. I can imagine their jaws dropping with each comparison. Up until that point, they had probably reckoned that they were doing quite well! Here are some of those challenges from Jesus, together with some imagined reactions from the disciples:

You have heard that it was said, 'Do not commit adultery.' But now I tell you: anyone who looks at a woman and wants to possess her is guilty of committing adultery with her in his heart." Matthew 5:27–28 (GNT)

"That's very hard, Jesus. What about my right to do anything I want to, as long as it doesn't harm anybody else?"

"You have heard that it was said, 'An eye for an eye, and a tooth for a tooth.' But now I tell you: do not take revenge on someone who wrongs you. If anyone slaps you on the right cheek, let him slap your left cheek too." Matthew 5:38–39 (GNT)

"Jesus, are You sure that's fair? What about my right of redress?"

"You have heard that it was said, 'Love your friends, hate your enemies.' But now I tell you: love your enemies and pray for those who persecute you." Matthew 5:43–44 (GNT)

"Jesus, that's crazy! What about my right to choose whom I like or don't like?"

Truly, without the mind of Christ operating in our lives

through the presence of the Holy Spirit, we cannot achieve the standards of behaviour consistent with the Kingdom of God, nor can we understand God's view of our rights. The covenant agreement of this Kingdom (as opposed to the social contracts in the world) requires a high level of righteousness amongst its citizens. This is impossible for us, but fully achieved by the One who represented us at the Cross, the place that this covenant was sealed between human beings and God. Wonderfully, if we surrender our lives completely to the commands of Jesus, He meets the requirements of this Kingdom on our behalf, and we have access to His way of thinking together with all the rights and privileges available as citizens and members of God's family.

God's answer for man's inhumanity to man

Jesus fully understands the oppression that exists in the world. He understands the genuine cry for freedom, justice and rights. He does not condemn those who fight for the victims of hatred. He understands the brokenness and bondage in people's lives. However, He stepped into this world and taught a new way for resolving the disorder. He taught about a Kingdom and obedience to the King who would never be an instrument of tyrannical persecution but would bring true peace and wellbeing.

> *"Happy are those who know they are spiritually poor; the Kingdom of heaven belongs to them! ... Happy are those who are persecuted because they do what God requires; the Kingdom of heaven belongs to them!" Matthew 5:3,10 (GNT)*

Jesus knows that we need provision and protection for our lives, but in His Kingdom, these are not won by aggressively pursuing self-proclaimed rights, but rather by quietly pursuing obedience to the ways of His Kingdom.

*"So do not start worrying: 'Where will my food come from?
Or my drink? Or my clothes?' (These are the things the pagans
are always concerned about.) Your Father in heaven knows
that you need all these things. Instead, be concerned above
everything else with the Kingdom of God and with what he
requires of you, and he will provide you with all these other
things." Matthew 6:31–33 (GNT)*

In summary

A social contract between rulers and those ruled, together with
associated citizens' rights, has a sensible purpose in each nation.
However, when nations covenant together in pursuance of a
faith in the ideology of universal human rights, that is a very
different matter. A covenant is a very serious agreement, one
might say even a matter of life and death. There is a spiritual
aspect to a covenant which holds the concerned parties to the
agreement in ways that can have far-reaching consequences.

God has always planned a covenant relationship with human
beings, initially revealed in detail to His chosen people, the
Jews. The evidence of the Bible is that they were unable to be
obedient to the terms of the divine covenant and therefore
unable to claim the fullness of God-given human rights. God
chose to establish a new extended covenant, now open to all,
through a perfect representative of God and of man, namely the
Son of God and the Son of Man, Jesus Christ.

God has not instructed human beings to enter into any
covenant, except within the context of marriage and of our
relationship with Him. However, many nations in the world
have chosen to bind themselves to each other in a covenant,
based on a belief that the ideology of universal human rights is
the ultimate answer to the injustice in the world. This ideology
may be well-meaning but it is a deception, and therefore God
cannot confer blessing through such a covenant.

In the next chapter we shall further consider the spiritual

consequence of claiming false human rights, and whether this man-made religion, internationally enshrined in covenantal agreements, should actually be regarded as a *doctrine of demons.*

Chapter 8

Universal human rights: a doctrine of demons?

Discerning the root from the fruit

Is it a step too far to say that rights ideology is being demonically promoted? Clearly, many advocates of human rights are honestly seeking to give voice to those who have genuinely suffered oppression and prejudice in this fallen world. However, human sincerity does not necessarily ensure freedom from spiritual deception. Sacrificial offerings made in pagan worship may be done with sincere belief in the efficacy of the practice, but the Bible makes it very clear that such sacrifice is made to demons alone (1 Corinthians 10:20).

The aggressive and irrational nature of some aspects of human rights activism, not least in the area of sexual rights, points far more to the character of the god of this world than to the grace and truth of Jesus. He teaches us to be very tolerant of each other's woundedness in the Body of Christ, but He also instructs us to be very intolerant of any wrong spirit that has been given licence to cause damage within His Body.

"But I have this against you, that you tolerate the woman Jezebel, who calls herself a prophetess, and she teaches and leads My bond-servants astray so that they commit acts of immorality and eat things sacrificed to idols." Revelation 2:20

God has given mankind a way to tackle the injustice of this world and His way is not the pursuance of rights. Jesus encourages us to look carefully at the fruit, the human disposition, in order to discern what spirit lies behind any movement or manifestation of power, however well-meaning the individuals involved may be.

"So then, you will know them by their fruits." Matthew 7:20

In more colloquial terms, I have to say that when I look at the ideology of universal human rights, I smell a rat. There is a control, a drivenness and a quasi-religious fervour associated with today's language of inclusivity, equality, freedom and rights that indicates spiritual energy far beyond just human motivation.

The Body of Christ is not called to fight against human beings, and certainly not against those with sincere intentions, but we are called to take issue with the spiritual powers and principalities that have deceived us and defiled human morality and justice.

For we are not fighting against human beings but against the wicked spiritual forces in the heavenly world, the rulers, authorities, and cosmic powers of this dark age. Ephesians 6:12 (GNT)

Understanding the deceptions of the enemy

But the Spirit explicitly says that in the later times some will fall away from the faith, paying attention to deceitful spirits and doctrines of demons. 1 Timothy 4:1

It has often been said that if the enemy's lies were obvious we wouldn't fall for them. Salmon get caught on a hook because it is concealed by a very attractive fly, albeit an artificial one. In the Garden of Eden, Satan makes a very attractive proposition: eating the forbidden fruit will give man divine knowledge. What could be wrong with that? But God had given a clear warning about disregarding His wisdom, declaring, "You will surely die." James says something equally strong to those depending on their own wisdom.

Are there any of you who are wise and understanding? You are to prove it by your good life, by your good deeds performed with humility and wisdom. But if in your heart you are jealous, bitter, and selfish, don't sin against the truth by boasting of your wisdom. Such wisdom does not come down from heaven; it belongs to the world, it is unspiritual and demonic. James 3:13–15 (GNT)

This is serious! When man boasts of his own wisdom, it can apparently become a doorway for the demonic realm. Secular humanism does exactly that. It boasts of man's ability to reason entirely out of his own intellect, without the need for God. Frequently, when people are claiming their rights, we see jealousy and selfishness at the root of the argument, because they perceive that others are perhaps receiving some form of privilege that they are not. Of course, those who are truly suffering oppression need our care and help to find justice, but a world that encourages the strident pursuing of entitlement quickly breeds discontentment and envy. When man alone decides what is just, he gives opportunity to the powers of darkness.

One of the reasons why the French Declaration of the Rights of Man, in 1789, proved to be such a spiritually significant moment was not only that God's sovereignty was completely ignored but, as we have noted, endorsement for the document was sought from an antichrist demonic spirit, named as the Supreme Being. This was, in effect, a welcome mat for the enemy to enter into the justice system of a nation, and indeed to infect all those nations that have subsequently used this pivotal declaration as a blueprint for producing similar constitutional statements. There is no doubt that the French declaration, however much it has been re-worked, has provided the foundation for much of today's faith in the efficacy of human rights.

The charge of discrimination – the world's response to God's view of sin

A rights-based system of justice neatly side-steps the need to directly confront the issue of sinful lifestyles. The enemy is content to seduce us onto this pathway, for, if the biblical concept of sin is no longer acknowledged, who needs a Saviour? Rather than permitting a genuine Christian challenge to particular beliefs and behaviours, the world favours combative accusation of anyone who does not accept another person's self-declared rights to a particular lifestyle. The accusations not infrequently end in the courtroom with charges of homophobia, transphobia, unlawful discrimination or even a hate crime.

If I dare to suggest that pornography, so readily available on the internet, is seriously polluting society, I am likely to be told that such a view is discrimination against every person's right to watch whatever sexual material they choose. If I dare to say that assisted suicide is contrary to the Word of God, many will say that this view is outdated and discriminates against someone's personal right to end suffering and life itself. If I dare to say that a child's wish to change gender appearance on the basis of troubled inner feelings is a denial of biological and biblical truth, many will say that this is discrimination against a child's right to a choice of gender identity.

Whilst the ostensible aim of those promoting unopposed acceptance of these personal rights is to end discrimination, the actual intention is to change the entire basis of society from one governed by extrinsic moral values and duties to one in which our only duty is to fulfil our own desires. This ideology clearly aligns itself with the god of this world and reminds us of the observation made in the Bible as to what happens when rightful authority is lost. The book of Judges finishes with these troubling words:

In those days there was no king in Israel; everyone did what was right in his own eyes. Judges 21:25

"Discrimination!" This is the frequent battle cry of many groups when faced with any questioning of their declared right to a particular lifestyle. The rights-based culture of our times has fostered the notion that to question a person's lifestyle is to discriminate against them as a fellow human being. Neither discrimination nor intolerance towards any category of people should be the attitude of anyone within the Body of Christ, but with grace we should be clear in our discrimination between what is right and what is wrong behaviour. Jesus was able to completely love the sinner but to clearly hate the sin.

I was amused to read the report of a speech by the Russian president Vladimir Putin, addressed to the Duma (the Russian

Parliament) in February 2013, highlighting the tensions with minorities in Russia:

> *All minorities should respect the Russian laws...we will not grant them special privileges, or try to change our laws to fit their desires, no matter how loud they yell 'discrimination'...*

The politicians in the Duma gave Putin a standing ovation for five minutes. It may not have been spoken with much grace by the president, but perhaps the Body of Christ should be more willing to say that, while unconditionally accepting each person whom God has created, discrimination against ungodly (perhaps minority) lifestyles is a necessary and loving aspect of the Gospel message, for God cannot change His laws to suit our preferences.

Hijacking the true source of justice is not new

Absalom wanted to hijack the authority of his father, King David, and gain favour with the people by endorsing the legal entitlements of those coming to see the king, without their having to face David's true justice. This, I believe, is exactly what the enemy is doing in these days as he aggressively promotes the universal rights of mankind in preference to divine justice.

I suggest that there is a powerful demonic spirit defiling the world today, of a character similar to that which operated through Absalom. It is a proud spirit seeking to seduce us away from true justice and morality, based on the wisdom of King Jesus, towards an alternative code of ethics, based only on man's wisdom. The latter is being made to seem particularly attractive because it avoids the uncomfortable issue of sin.

Then Absalom would say to him, "See, your claims are good and right, but no man listens to you on the part of the king." Moreover, Absalom would say, "Oh that one would appoint me judge in the land; then every man who has any suit or cause could come to me and I would give him justice." 2 Samuel 15:3–4

Without a true, divine arbiter of sin, morality and justice, we simply become a society competing with our individual claims of entitlement, so that the strongest, the most eloquent, the loudest or the most influential people become the ones who eventually decide what is to be regarded as right or wrong. This dismissal of God's wisdom and of His order means that the enemy grows in his authority and therefore in his control over the life of humankind (Ephesians 2:1–3). He is very content to receive whatever rights we give him to extend his world rule!

Understanding spiritual authority and power

Delegated authority confers a *right* to carry out some particular action. Power provides the *ability* to carry out that action. Ian

Fleming's famous fictional character James Bond, the British secret agent code-named 007, was given a licence to kill certain targeted individuals. Laying aside the very doubtful morality of this delegated authority, we can say the Mr Bond had a right to take life, but he also needed the ability to carry out murder through the power of a gun or similar weapon.

Ever since the fall of humankind, Satan and his realm of darkness have had the ability, the power, to adversely affect human lives; in fact, Jesus refers to Satan as a murderer. God had originally created and empowered these spiritual beings to serve His good purposes, in obedience to His commands. However, they rebelled against God and lost the given right, the authority, to use the power with which they had been endowed. The only means of their securing a licence to operate is now by the rights that humans give them through their obedience to the ways of the ruler of the world, and consequently their disobedience to the Creator of the Universe.

Human sin gives the enemy rights to use demonic power to control, damage and destroy human life. The enemy's licence to control and even murder comes not from his Creator, but from sinners like you and me! Jesus explained to the Pharisees that their following of the ways of the enemy inevitably gave him destructive oversight of their lives.

> *"You are the children of your father, the Devil, and you want to follow your father's desires. From the very beginning he was a murderer..." John 8:44a (GNT)*

The danger of claiming illegitimate rights

I am declaring something very serious here. The more that man claims universal and inalienable *human* rights, contrary to the truth of scripture, the more he increases the *demonic* rights of the enemy. Satan and his domain have no authority to operate in our lives apart from the entitlement that we give him by ignoring the Word of God. It started in the Garden of Eden, when Adam and Eve, through their obedience to the instruction of Satan, transferred the authority which God had given to them over to this deceiving serpent. And this giving over of man's legitimate rights to spiritually rule the earth to the powers of darkness has continued to this day. All spiritual authority that exists in the universe originates from God, but much delegated authority has ended up, through man's disobedience, entitling the enemy to control human life.

When, for example, I claim a personal right to use recreational drugs and alter my body chemistry, I am acting as my own god in agreement with the nature of the enemy. I am acting in opposition to God who created me, the One who has declared my extraordinary innate value. In consequence, I give the powers of darkness a right to control that aspect of my life, meaning that the bondage of addiction is not just chemical but spiritual. In the same way, I make myself spiritually vulnerable through any right that I claim which is not consistent with the word of God: a right to retribution, a right to sexual intimacy outside biblical marriage, a right to abort an unwanted foetus, a right to change my gender appearance, a right to blaspheme against God.

Of course, we each have the *ability* to do any of these things, but God has not conferred any *right* to such activity. In fact, He seeks, through the Bible and through the guidance of the Holy Spirit, to strongly dissuade us from every sinful action that is likely to damage our lives. When we act contrary to His ways, and walk according to the rights advocated by secular humanism, we don't gain any legitimate spiritual authority over our lives, but rather we give it away to the ruler of the world. Isaiah gave witness to the fact that the spirit operating in the king of Babylon was eagerly driving this arrogant king's self-proclamation of entitlement, a rebellious behaviour which was to inevitably end in the king's destruction.

You were determined to climb up to heaven and to place your throne above the highest stars. You thought you would sit like a king on that mountain in the north where the gods assemble. You said you would climb to the tops of the clouds and be like the Almighty. But instead, you have been brought down to the deepest part of the world of the dead. Isaiah 14:13–15 (GNT)

Who gets the upper hand in the battle of rights?

In his letter to the church at Corinth, Paul explains this problem of how the enemy gains a right to control our lives. Clearly someone has been causing upset in the congregation, and Paul is concerned that both he and those in the church need to speak out forgiveness. He knows very well that unforgiveness, and claiming a right of redress, are contrary to the ways of God and give a clear opportunity for the enemy to assume destructive spiritual authority among the believers. The Good News Bible has an interesting way of translating Paul's concerns about Satan being given rights over those in the church.

> *When you forgive people for what they have done, I forgive them too. For when I forgive – if, indeed, I need to forgive anything – I do it in Christ's presence because of you, in order to keep Satan from getting the upper hand over us; for we know what his plans are. 2 Corinthians 2:10–11 (GNT)*

Anyone who has the *upper hand* has authority over others, a right to exercise control, and this is exactly what Paul fears if unforgiveness continues. When Satan rebelled against God he lost the delegated divine authority to exercise his power. Ever since the Fall, he has looked for any opportunity to receive authority through man's disagreement with God and his acquiescence to the seductive temptations of the world. Satan understands his rights and knows that rebellious humans provide the only source of authority he can claim to damage their lives.

The declaration, promotion and protection of universal human rights is a plausible philosophy for seeking justice and morality in this disordered world. However, if the concept is inconsistent with God's way of justice, the eventual result will be lawlessness rather than social order. The truth of man's inalienable value has been distorted by the lie of man's inalienable rights. Pressing for these individual rights leads, more often than not, to dispute rather than peace.

Satan completely understands the issue of delegated rights. He knows that true entitlement must be conferred by one who has the authority to delegate. The religious leaders around Jesus were furious at His authoritative presence and challenged Him on the legitimacy of His right to say such things. They, and the powers of darkness working through them, wanted to retain the upper hand of control over the people.

Jesus came back to the Temple; and as he taught, the chief priests and the elders came to him and asked, "What right do you have to do these things? Who gave you such right?"
Matthew 21:23 (GNT)

We see here a clear example of the foundational clash between the destructive rights claimed by the enemy through the sinfulness of man, and the life-giving rights of Jesus to impart truth into a damaged world. God has ultimate authority to release true rights to mankind through Jesus Christ, but the ruler of this world will do all he can to oppose that authority by deceiving and intimidating humankind into adopting false teaching, false ideologies, false justice and false rights.

The enemy's strategy of plausibility

Secular humanism rests on a belief that human assessment should be the final arbiter of conscience. Of course, common sense is not always bad, but followers of Jesus need to remember that God thinks very differently from human beings, and our senses have been seriously defiled by sin.

"For My thoughts are not your thoughts, nor are your ways My ways," declares the LORD. Isaiah 55:8

Our thinking is distorted by a sinful nature that easily slips into believing that the wisdom of human beings must be sufficient for the ordering of this world. However, as we have seen, the enemy's methods of deception often mean that lies are concealed within an appearance of truth. The plausibility of a belief in universal human rights can be the enemy's most seductive weapon against those who challenge its validity.

Thomas Paine, the Enlightenment philosopher whom I mentioned previously, wrote a book called *Common Sense*, in which he maintained that the corruption of church and state are best counteracted by letting justice flow from the combined will of the people. His very reasonable arguments advocated the abandoning of traditional concepts of divine authority in favour of human intellect and rights, but he ended his days in sad disillusionment. Here are some thoughts on the apparent plausibility of universal human rights ideology.

Human rights surely empower people against unjust government. The ideology of human rights is simply a man-made concept, able to be altered or ignored at any time by a government. It is better to challenge the wrongfulness of any oppressive state control directly, and to seek better structures of government accountability. The horror of the French guillotine and the Reign of Terror was certainly no endorsement for the belief that declaring the inalienable rights of citizens necessarily empowers a people against its leaders.

Every human being, no matter their social status, can at least claim their fundamental rights. Everyone, no matter their position in society, should indeed be allowed to have a voice to seek what is fair. However, the concept of universal rights means that claims can be, and frequently are, made by those who have no intention of exercising a needful responsibility within society. In fact, the relentless promotion of rights seems very often to just encourage selfishness rather than bring true justice.

Promoting human rights is an internationally recognised solution for ending conflict between nations. It may be the place of faith for many nations, but the evidence for the true effectiveness of a rights-based world justice system is hard to find. The arrogance of many leaders pursuing rights for themselves and their nation appears to have increased conflict around the world rather than to have lessened it. The right to nuclear weapons for self-defence is a pertinent example.

The ideology of human rights avoids the need for any religious conviction in the promotion of justice. Unless a system of justice is grounded in something beyond mere human reason, it carries very doubtful long-term authority or stability, being vulnerable to constant change with fashion or politics. Followers of Jesus may not necessarily be able to change political thinking, but we can at least hold up the unchanging plumb-line of God's Word, and make known the true source of justice and wellbeing for humanity.

Pursuing human rights is the best means of safeguarding human freedom. We must ask the question, "What exactly is freedom?" The secular humanist would say that it is the unrestrained ability for each individual to express his or her own personality and ambition, but this puts no boundary on our behaviour within society. Jesus, however, tells us that everyone who commits sin is a slave to sin (John 8:34). God has secured our liberty from this spiritual slavery through our confessing of wrongdoing, and this is true freedom.

With God's help, we need to discern what strategies the ruler of this world is working on behind the scenes, in trying to undermine God's plans for the redemption of humanity. God wants us to reason with Him and not just rely on what seems reasonable or plausible according to our own assessment. We have a vicious enemy.

The Plan of Alice Bailey

I recently came across the writings of a lady called Alice Bailey. It seemed to me that here was an important glimpse behind the scenes into just one of the many unseen strategies of the enemy, over the last century, to undermine biblical Christianity and to press home the ideology of humanism and rights into a spiritually naïve world.

Alice Bailey (1880–1949), although not a well-known authoress, has been described by some as 'the mother of the New Age'. In the 1920s, at the dictation of a spirit guide, according to her record, she wrote *The Plan*, a systematic programme to, in her view, liberate the world from the restrictions of Christianity. Here are some key points from that plan for a new world order:

Push God out of schools.

Break the traditional Judeo-Christian family concept.
Break communication between parents and children,
so that parents will not pass on spiritual values to their
children. Achieve this by promoting excessive child rights.

Remove restrictions on sex. Sex is the biggest joy in life,
and everyone should be free to enjoy it without restrictions.
People must be free to enjoy sex in all its forms.

Homosexuality should be on an equal level as
heterosexuality.

Abortion is a human right.

In order to find happiness, you must join together with any person with whom a bond develops, whether they are married or not.

Diffuse religious radicalism, by silencing Christianity and promoting other faiths. Also, after the other faiths have become strong, silence them, and create interfaith harmony.
Use the media to influence and create mass opinion.
Debase art in all its forms – make it obscene, immoral, occultic.

Make the Church endorse every one of these changes.

Whether or not this plan was ever taken seriously by the readers of Alice Bailey, or given a practical outworking by any of her followers, the ongoing and astonishing fulfilment of this humanistic and defiling agenda reminds me that the enemy gets a significant measure of spiritual license from the rebellious ways of human beings.

In summary
The world has decided to vigorously self-proclaim innate rights, without the need for a divine covenant, and that is no different from a hijacker on a plane using force to claim his right to control the flight. Any belief or activity that denies the true authority of God gives a right to the enemy.

The fruit of rights activism very often bears the irrational and aggressive character of the enemy, the god of this world, rather than the gracious character of Jesus. If the religion of universal human rights does indeed contradict the Word of God in regard to true justice, then Satan can empower the licence that humanity has given him. He can promote the doctrine with the aid of demons.

The Body of Christ is not in a fight against people, often well-meaning people who nevertheless may have been deceived by a worthless ideology, but we are called to be intolerant of the spiritual powers that operate under the cover of deceptive philosophies, and the Bible tells us to take care that we are not taken captive by such things. Our journey with Jesus is not a walk in the park but a trek across a very hostile spiritual battlefield.

See to it, then, that no one enslaves you by means of the worthless deceit of human wisdom, which comes from the teachings handed down by human beings and from the ruling spirits of the universe, and not from Christ. Colossians 2:8 (GNT)

In the Garden of Eden, Satan said to our ancestors, "Ignore God's instructions, eat the fruit, it won't harm you." And they fell for it, quite literally. Today, he says, "Ignore God's instructions; justify your sin by calling it a human right."

And we are still falling for it.

Chapter 9

True God-given Rights

God's plan of true rights from the moment of creation

I started this book by making this statement: the ideology of universal human rights offers a false hope of true justice and peace in this very damaged and hurting world. In the Body of Christ, we need to be very careful that, in our compassion for the hurting, we do not fall into the trap of promoting man's rights at the expense of ignoring man's sin. The peace that the world desires will never come without heeding the truth of God's Word. I trust that I have sufficiently explained my reasons for making that initial statement. I also said that I hoped to give direction to the only true pathway of justice and restoration for humankind. It is this hope that is the purpose of this chapter.

However much Thomas Jefferson, in composing the United States Declaration of Independence, wished to believe that God had conferred inalienable rights on every human being from birth, the fact remains that he chose to ignore the consequence of sin. Without the Fall we would indeed be dwelling in divinely imparted rights, but we need to look at the reality of what the Bible actually says. It is important to remind ourselves that, in the context of what is being discussed in this book, a legitimate right can be described as *conferred* authority, a given entitlement or privilege, and it can only be granted by someone with a valid *higher* authority.

We have considered the relationship between covenants and rights. God's plan for His creation has always been that there would be a covenant relationship between Him, our Heavenly Father, and ourselves as His children. Within this covenant He planned the conferring of rights, in particular the delegating of divine authority together with an enabling power, for humans to rule over His creation. God alone has the authority to confer rights to each human life that He has created. Indeed, before the Fall He had released a significant measure of authority and privilege:

- A right to exercise dominion over the earth and its animals, on behalf of God:
  [God] blessed them, and said, "Have many children, so that your descendants will live all over the earth and bring it under their control. I am putting you in charge of the fish, the birds, and all the wild animals." Genesis 1:28 (GNT)
- A right to take everlasting spiritual nourishment from the Tree of Life:
  He made all kinds of beautiful trees grow there and produce good fruit. In the middle of the garden stood the tree that gives life... Genesis 2:9a (GNT)

- A right to cultivate the land in order to promote order and fruitfulness:
  ... Then the LORD God placed the man in the Garden of Eden to cultivate it and guard it. Genesis 2:15 (GNT)
- A right to name the animals:
  So he took some soil from the ground and formed all the animals and all the birds. Then he brought them to the man to see what he would name them; and that is how they all got their names. Genesis 2:19 (GNT)
- A right to the spiritual covering of God, irrespective of physical nakedness.
  And the man and his wife were both naked and were not ashamed. Genesis 2:25
- A right to freely take from plants and trees all that was needed for food.
  He told him [Adam], "You may eat the fruit of any tree in the garden." Genesis 2:16 (GNT)

These can be summed up as God giving humankind a right, at the point of creation, to an abundant life by means of His provision and protection. However, in the same way that a fisherman who has been given fishing rights on a stretch of water must stay within the boundaries of that permission, so God put an important boundary on His conferring of rights to human beings in the Garden:

"...except the tree that gives knowledge of what is good and what is bad. You must not eat the fruit of that tree; if you do, you will die the same day." Gen 2:17 (GNT)

Man's choice of rebellion

Because He only wanted a true relationship with those whom He had created, God gave humankind the ability to disobey Him, a freewill choice to say *yes* or *no* to the terms of the divine covenant. Unfortunately, starting with our first ancestors, we have ignored God's stated boundaries and broken covenant with our Maker.

> *But like Adam they have transgressed the covenant; there they have dealt treacherously against Me. Hosea 6:7*

In so doing, humankind lost all the rights God had given through the covenant agreement, in particular the entitlement to eternal and abundant life together with his Maker, the right of access to the Tree of Life.

> *Then the LORD God said, "Now these human beings have become like one of us and have knowledge of what is good and what is bad. They must not be allowed to take fruit from the tree that gives life, eat it, and live forever." Genesis 3:22 (GNT)*

Without the solution of the Cross, that would have remained the condition of humankind. Without a covenant relationship with God, we had no innate rights, because sin had cancelled them out. In fact, the situation was worse than that. Not only did man disobey God, he followed the instruction of a powerful spiritual being in the Garden, Satan. By accepting Satan's authority over his life rather than God's authority, the right of dominion over the earth was handed over to a new ruler of the world. We see the reality of the entitlement given to this ruler during the temptation of Jesus.

> *The devil led him [Jesus] up to a high place and showed him in an instant all the kingdoms of the world. And he said to him, "I will give you all their authority and splendour; it has been given to me, and I can give it to anyone I want to." Luke 4:5–6 (NIV)*

God's evolving plan to restore covenant with man

After the Fall, in order to restore human beings' rights as members of His family and citizens of His Kingdom, God embarked on a long journey of explanation and instruction concerning the laws governing His creation, and how we could benefit from these laws by walking in covenant obedience to Him.

Noah certainly understood that a covenant relationship with God, and the privilege of life for himself and his family, were quite literally dependent on persistent obedience to God's commands, in particular the requirement to build a life-saving boat.

> *"...but I will make a covenant with you. Go into the boat with your wife, your sons, and their wives. Take into the boat with you a male and a female of every kind of animal and of every kind of bird, in order to keep them alive. Take along all kinds of food for you and for them." Noah did everything that God commanded. Genesis 6:18–22 (GNT)*

God later chose Abraham in order to initiate a special divine covenant, an extraordinary agreement with him and his descendants. This covenant, specifically with the Jewish people, gave them rights to divine protection and provision, including the remarkable allocation of particular land. As we have previously noted, there were requirements upon the people to walk in obedience.

> *"I will keep my promise to you and to your descendants in future generations as an everlasting covenant. I will be your God and the God of your descendants. I will give to you and to your descendants this land in which you are now a foreigner.... You and your descendants must all agree to circumcise every male among you." Genesis 17:7–8a,10 (GNT)*

There was also an important principle reflected in the concept of birth-right, a means of godly privilege and blessing passed on from a father to his children, but sometimes lost through sinful behaviour.

> *When Esau heard the words of his father, he cried out with an exceedingly great and bitter cry, and said to this father, "Bless me, even me also, O my father!" And he [Isaac] said, "Your brother came deceitfully and has taken away your blessing." Then he [Esau] said, "Is he not rightfully named Jacob, for he has supplanted me these two times? He took away my birth right, and behold, now he has taken away my blessing." Genesis 27:34–36*

The terms and benefits of the divine covenant with the Children of Israel were later revealed in more detail through Moses. God further explained the spiritual laws of His Kingdom and gave them clear commandments how to keep in line with these laws, and so enjoy the privileges of His provision and protection in this special covenant.

> *"If you live according to my laws and obey my commands, I will send you rain at the right time, so that the land will produce crops and the trees will bear fruit. Your crops will be so plentiful that you will still be harvesting grain when it is time to pick grapes, and you will still be picking grapes when it is time to plant grain. You will have all that you want to eat, and you can live in safety in your land. I will give you peace in your land, and you can sleep without being afraid of anyone. I will get rid of the dangerous animals in the land, and there will be no more war there." Leviticus 26:3–6 (GNT)*

If they obeyed the conditions of this covenant relationship, they would be able to claim a foundational right to be God's chosen people.

I will be with you; I will be your God, and you will be my people. Leviticus 26:12 (GNT)

He also instructed them in how to be restored and cleansed following their inevitable and frequent disobedience, in particular through the Day of Atonement each year.

...for it is on this day that atonement shall be made for you to cleanse you; you will be clean from all your sins before the LORD. Leviticus 16:30

Through all this interaction between God and His chosen people, the Jews, He set in place a framework of justice and morality completely different from that of the pagan world around them. He chose this particular ethnic group to explain that, in covenant with Him, human beings could enjoy a right to know Him as their Father, provided they remained within the boundaries, the commandments which He gave them.

Do you thus repay the LORD, O foolish and unwise people? Is He not your Father who has bought you? He has made you and established you. Deuteronomy 32:6

God's final plan of restored covenant and rights for mankind

We read in the book of Jeremiah that God began to point His chosen people, the Children of Israel, to a time when there would be a new covenant.

The new covenant that I will make with the people of Israel will be this: I will put my law within them and write it on their hearts. I will be their God, and they will be my people. Jeremiah 31:33 (GNT)

This new divine covenant would not just be with the Jewish people, but with the whole of humankind, if they agreed to receive the truth and the Kingship of the promised Messiah, the One that was to be called Jesus.

"I, the LORD, have called you [the Messiah Jesus] and given you power to see that justice is done on earth. Through you I will make a covenant with all peoples; through you I will bring light to the nations." Isaiah 42:6 (GNT)

Isaiah prophesied that it would be a covenant that would confer the privilege of true restoration and freedom, which the world had so long needed:

He has sent me to bind up the broken-hearted, to proclaim liberty to captives, and freedom to prisoners. Isaiah 61:1b

Today, every human being has the opportunity to be a citizen of a divine Kingdom, where Jesus is King. Through Him, and through the new covenant which He has set in place between God and humankind, our true foundational rights can indeed be restored. Sadly, many have declined the offer, but, from the time of Jesus walking the earth, millions of people have said, "We believe!"

Some, however, did receive him [Jesus] and believed in him; so he gave them the right to become God's children. John 1:12 (GNT)

What an entitlement! This is the same foundational right that was promised to the Children of Israel, to know God as their Father. The Greek word, translated here as *right*, is *exousia*, meaning a delegated authority or privilege conferred by God on every person that surrenders to the Kingship of Jesus. Surely this verse is one of the most profound contained within the Bible. Without doubt, the enemy wants to hijack this true human right, and he would like humankind to believe that we do not need Jesus in order to claim our foundational rights, but he is a liar. A true framework of human justice and morality can only be set by our Creator, God Himself, and we have the freewill choice to obey or disobey. God has certainly not instructed humankind to determine his own set of self-proclaimed rights or his own code of morality.

The book of Revelation picks up the same truth: there can be restoration of foundational human rights lost at the Fall, for us to be eternal members of God's family. However, this is only through a covenant with God, by receiving Jesus Christ as King, and through our being cleansed from all unrighteousness.

Happy are those who wash their robes clean and so have the right to eat the fruit from the tree of life and to go through the gates into the city. Revelation 22:14 (GNT)

What is more, Satan, the one who seeks to deceive humankind into handing over the authority that God has purposed for us, is now under judgement through the coming of Jesus and the work of the Holy Spirit.

...and they [the people of the world] are wrong about judgment, because the ruler of this world has already been judged. John 16:11 (GNT)

The opportunity of true human rights

The prophet Isaiah saw the true source of justice in this world, through the One who would come by God's anointing.

Behold, My Servant, whom I uphold; My chosen one in whom My soul delights. I have put My Spirit upon Him; He will bring forth justice to the nations. Isaiah 42:1

As He walked the earth, Jesus surrendered His equality and privileges within the Godhead to the will of the Father (Philippians 2:5–11). He could have claimed absolute entitlement to man's immediate submission, but He chose only to act on the authority delegated to Him for the task of man's redemption.

At the Cross, Jesus paid the penalty for sin, He established a new covenant between God and man, He made it possible for us to receive forgiveness and healing, and He also made it possible for the rights which God had always desired to confer on to human beings to be restored to those willing to participate in His Kingdom. We have seen that the most important and foundational right is the extraordinary privilege of being a part of God's family, to truly know God as our Father. Every entitlement we have, as followers of Jesus, flows from this key human right that has been conferred by the will of Almighty God and not by the will of man.

As God's children, and citizens of His kingdom, we can enjoy an entitlement to this divine relationship that can indeed be described as inalienable, because nothing can separate us from the love of our Father.

For I am certain that nothing can separate us from his love: neither death nor life, neither angels nor other heavenly rulers or powers, neither the present nor the future, neither the world above nor the world below – there is nothing in all creation that will ever be able to separate us from the love of God which is ours through Christ Jesus our Lord. Rom 8:38–39 (GNT)

Wonderful! It is this security that the heart of every human desires, but without Jesus it remains just a deep and unattainable longing. The human spirit of every person that has ever lived was designed to know this intimate covenant relationship with the One who created that spirit, but sadly the world has largely rejected the only way to know the Father; that is, through receiving Jesus Christ as Lord of our lives.

Jesus answered him, "I am the way, the truth, and the life; no one goes to the Father except by me." John 14:6 (GNT)

We have seen that covenant agreements always give rights to the participants, and the New Covenant is no exception. God has supreme authority and therefore holds every right according to His choice, but He has also chosen to confer specific rights to mankind within the boundaries of covenant.

The world has sought to claim such innate rights – to life, freedom, and the pursuit of happiness, for example – without acknowledging the need for divine conferral. It is fully understandable, but it is biblically illegitimate. The world chooses to believe that there are inalienable rights simply by virtue of being born a human being. The Bible is clear that we only have such innate rights as a result of being born *again* of the Spirit of God, through receiving Jesus. This is the only way to become a citizen in the Kingdom of God and to benefit from the rights of that citizenship.

"I am telling you the truth," replied Jesus, "that no one can enter the Kingdom of God without being born of water and the Spirit. A person is born physically of human parents, but is born spiritually of the Spirit. Do not be surprised because I tell you that you must all be born again." John 3:5–7 (GNT)

Citizens' rights to an eternal Kingdom

When we receive Jesus as Lord and Saviour, we enter a realm of spiritual light and receive the foundational right of being a member of God's family. We are given an eternal "passport" which states that we are citizens of the Kingdom of Heaven.

For our citizenship is in heaven, from which also we eagerly wait for a Savior, the Lord Jesus Christ. Philippians 3:20

Jesus tells His disciples that, despite the remarkable authority which He has delegated to them to overcome the power of the enemy, it is their identity in His Kingdom that is the most important right conferred.

"Listen! I have given you authority, so that you can walk on snakes and scorpions and overcome all the power of the Enemy, and nothing will hurt you. But don't be glad because the evil spirits obey you; rather be glad because your names are written in heaven." Luke 10:19–20 (GNT)

Discovering the privileges

The first disciples discovered a remarkable array of rights, by way of delegated authority, entitlements and privileges, which flowed from this new covenant position. These are specific rights that we all now have through the key right of being God's children, provided that we walk in obedience to the boundaries set by the Giver of those rights. I previously said that all the rights which were lost at the Fall could be summarised as the granting of God's provision and protection. Through Jesus there is a wonderful redemption of what was lost, so let's affirm some of the rights that Jesus Himself promised to confer on all His disciples:

- A right to fullness of life:
  "The thief comes only in order to steal, kill, and destroy. I have come in order that you might have life – life in all its fullness". John 10:10 (GNT)
- A right to eternal life and freedom from judgement:
  "I am telling you the truth: those who hear my words and believe in him who sent me have eternal life. They will not be judged, but have already passed from death to life." John 5:24 (GNT)
- A right or privilege to know truth and freedom:
  So Jesus said to those who believed in him, "If you obey my teaching, you are really my disciples; you will know the truth, and the truth will set you free." John 8:31–32 (GNT)
- A right to have prayers answered:
  "If you believe, you will receive whatever you ask for in prayer." Matt 21:22 (GNT)
- A right or an authority to overcome the power of the enemy:
  "Listen! I have given you authority, so that you can walk on snakes and scorpions and overcome all the power of the Enemy, and nothing will hurt you." Luke 10:19 (GNT)
- A right or privilege of bearing fruit, the character of Jesus:
  "I am the vine, and you are the branches. Those who remain in me, and I in them, will bear much fruit; for you can do nothing without me." John 15:5 (GNT)
- A right to receive God's forgiveness as we forgive others:
  "If you forgive others the wrongs they have done to you, your Father in heaven will also forgive you." Matthew 6:14 (GNT)
- A right or privilege to know the secrets of the Kingdom of Heaven:
  Then the disciples came to Jesus and asked him, "Why do you use parables when you talk to the people?" Jesus answered, "The knowledge about the secrets of the Kingdom of heaven has been given to you, but not to them." Matthew 13:10–11 (GNT)

- A right to pronounce the binding or loosing of spiritual authority:
  "Truly I say to you, whatever you bind on earth shall have been bound in heaven; and whatever you loose on earth shall have been loosed in heaven." Matthew 18:18
- A right to inner peace:
  "Come to Me, all who are weary and heavy-laden, and I will give you rest. Take My yoke upon you and learn from Me, for I am gentle and humble in heart, and YOU WILL FIND REST FOR YOUR SOULS." Matthew 11:28
- A right or privilege to receive the Holy Spirit:
  "As bad as you are, you know how to give good things to your children. How much more, then, will the Father in heaven give the Holy Spirit to those who ask him!" Luke 11:13 (GNT)
- A right to divine wisdom:
  "Make up your minds ahead of time not to worry about how you will defend yourselves, because I will give you such words and wisdom that none of your enemies will be able to refute or contradict what you say." Luke 21:14–15 (GNT)
- A right to the continual presence of Jesus:
  "Go, then, to all peoples everywhere and make them my disciples: baptize them in the name of the Father, the Son, and the Holy Spirit, and teach them to obey everything I have commanded you. And I will be with you always, to the end of the age." Matthew 28:19–20 (GNT)

But be careful!

There needs to be a word of warning. These rights in God's Kingdom will never be the result of our personal merit or righteousness, but rather they are the consequence of the grace of God and the sacrifice of Jesus at the Cross. Furthermore, the enjoyment of these rights listed above is wholly dependent on adherence to the conditions under which they have been conferred.

The more a person claims rights without obedience to the

Giver of those rights, the less true authority he or she will carry. We do not lose our citizenship in Britain by dangerous driving, but we may well lose our right to take a car on the British roads (our driving licence). In a similar way, as believers in Jesus, we are secure in our citizenship in the Kingdom of God, but the legitimacy of divinely conferred rights is dependent upon our day-to-day surrender to the King.

> *"And I [Jesus] will do whatever you ask for in my name, so that the Father's glory will be shown through the Son. If you ask me for anything in my name, I will do it. If you love me, you will obey my commandments." John 14:13–15 (GNT)*

We need to remember that there is an enemy who will continually contest our Kingdom rights, by seeking to tempt us and expose any weakness that exists in our relationship with Jesus. We can see the strength of this contest in the satanic challenge to the apostle Peter, revealed by Jesus.

> *"Simon, Simon! Listen! Satan has received permission to test all of you, to separate the good from the bad, as a farmer separates the wheat from the chaff." Luke 22:31 (GNT)*

The good news is that Jesus is fighting for us to strengthen us, to forgive us, to cleanse us and restore our place of legitimate entitlement in God's family.

> *"But I [Jesus] have prayed for you, Simon, that your faith will not fail. And when you turn back to me, you must strengthen your brothers." Luke 22:32 (GNT)*

However, like Peter, we need to be willing to acknowledge our weaknesses and confess our sins, in order to confront the accusation of the enemy and be free from his grip on any part of our lives. Freedom comes not by claiming my rights, however wounded I have been, but by forgiving those who have wounded me and acknowledging my own wrongful beliefs and behaviours.

But if we confess our sins to God, he will keep his promise and do what is right: he will forgive us our sins and purify us from all our wrongdoing. 1 John 1:9 (GNT)

By way of an example, if I am bound by self-hatred as a consequence of abuse in my life, it is so important that I bring this painful issue to Jesus. He knows the reasons for my thoughts and feelings and He does not condemn me. But His unconditional love for me and my deep-seated hatred of myself are not in agreement, so the enemy has a right to challenge my entitlement to peace, and he has a right to hold a measure of spiritual control over that part of my life. However, as I understand the truth and the source of my pain, I have the opportunity to forgive those who abused me, to confess the sin of self-rejection, and to be fully in agreement with the King!

This may take time, but when it happens the accusation of the enemy has to stop, his licence to control is revoked, I can be free from his spiritual hold, and as I am restored to the fullness of my rights as a child of God, inner peace will surely come.

In summary

True human rights do exist! Beyond the limited entitlements and duties that are necessarily agreed between governments and citizens, God has always intended that every created human being should be able to enjoy foundational rights conferred by Him, ensuring the provision and protection of a Heavenly Father. However, these rights are divinely ordained to exist only within the boundary of a covenant relationship with Him. Sadly, man is by nature a covenant breaker. Even the Children of Israel, a people clearly set apart to demonstrate God's faithfulness to humankind, repeatedly disobeyed the terms of the covenant which He made with them. God's final plan was to extend a covenant relationship beyond the Jewish people to the whole of humankind. However, this was only possible by sending Jesus, the Son of God, to represent the Godhead, in forming a new covenant. He represented mankind also, as the sinless Son of Man, fully obedient to Father God and willing to shed His blood at the Cross. He was able to reinstate both a new covenant and true human rights.

Such rights can be enjoyed by everyone who acknowledges Jesus as their personal representative at the Cross. Only by receiving Him and the truth of His words can we claim that we have a right to be children of God and to know all the amazing privileges which this right includes.

Chapter 10

Conclusion

The religion of universal human rights

On the BBC radio programme *A Point of View* in December 2013, the philosopher and political commentator John Gray, who describes himself as someone without religious beliefs, expressed concern about the religious nature of the ideology of rights. The talk was entitled *Two Cheers for Human Rights*. Here are a few of the inciteful comments that he made:

> *When we hear reports of nightmarish atrocities... it's easy to respond by thinking these horrors could be prevented if only the country had a government that respected human rights. We've come to believe rights are the answer to many of the world's ills. But rights aren't a cure to human conflict, and I think it's a mistake to treat them as an article of faith...*

Unless rights are grounded in something beyond the human world, they can only be a human invention. As someone without any religious beliefs that's a conclusion I'm happy to accept, but it has uncomfortable consequences for those who think human rights have universal authority...

Many people seem to think that once tyranny is demolished, human rights will emerge naturally from the rubble. But rights are artefacts of civilisation, not a natural human condition. If they protect us against the state, they are also created and enforced by states. Where the state is weak or collapsed, as in many parts of the world today, human rights simply don't exist...

Believers in human rights think the same as religious evangelists. Both are engaged in an unending project of conversion...

God says that, for the wellbeing of society, each person should acknowledge their wrongs, find His forgiveness and be at peace with one another. It seems that the world is increasingly saying that each person should claim their rights, be in competition with one another, and decide who is the greater victim.

In the lecture previously mentioned, to the Heritage Foundation in Washington in October 2015, Sir Roger Scruton commented:

The notion of a human right purports to offer the ground for moral opinions, for legal precepts, for policies designed to establish order in places where people are in competition and conflict. However, it is itself without foundations.

"My rights!" This ubiquitous human cry today is the consequence of man's search for justice but without reference to God's point of view. The promotion of so-called universal human rights may indeed be well-meaning, but it is not consistent with the Word of God. He has made it clear that, in His Kingdom, true rights are solely dependent on obedience to a covenant relationship with Him, through Jesus. He came to deal with sin, the reason we lost the rights God gave to us at creation. Humankind's problems result not from the absence of human rights but the presence of human sin.

The religion of rights contaminates every aspect of human life, not least the confusion that exists in the world over the precious innate identity that God has imparted to every human being. A man called Dean Bailey, in an interview with Pete Baklinski for LifeSiteNews in October 2014, candidly spoke about his journey of restoration from a homosexual lifestyle. He includes these comments:

> *The reality of this entire issue is that homosexuality is another human brokenness, a harmful behaviour pattern, and not a human identity or a human right... What they [gay activists] fear most is the breakdown and destruction of the inward lies that form the foundation of their own 'gay' identity, and everything that the 'gay rights' movement has been built upon.*

The challenge to the religion of universal human rights advocated in this book should never be an excuse for condemning and further rejecting those who truly are victims of intolerance, prejudice and bigotry. When the Church embraces the radical, loving inclusivity of Jesus towards every person, no matter their beliefs and lifestyle, we then win the right to teach the exclusivity of the Kingdom of God in regard to every belief and lifestyle that is not consistent with God's commands, for the sake of each person's true wellbeing.

Respecting the value of every person is entirely biblical because that value has been clearly affirmed by God. However, being required to respect their right, for example, to walk in a sinful lifestyle, is very different, as it begs the question, "By whom was that right conferred?" A right is not the same as an ability. In the story of the woman caught in adultery, in John chapter 8, Jesus showed His radical inclusion of all people, as He said, "I do not condemn you." However, in this place of true lovingkindness, He was enabled to declare an uncompromising exclusion of a wrongful lifestyle, in saying, "Do not sin anymore."

God's answer of true rights

The existence of true human rights is not simply the consequence of our *physical birth*, as the world chooses to claim, but rather the consequence of our *spiritual rebirth* into God's family. Without doubt, we all have extraordinary innate value and ability (Psalm 139:13–16), but God alone has the authority to confer legitimate rights to man. His distribution of given rights will never result in competition, as do our self-proclaimed rights, for His rights build His Body on earth and will not divide it.

Jesus not only explained the true meaning of God's laws as He walked on the earth, but He also fulfilled them. He showed in Himself the way God sees the issues of authority and rights. He did not exercise His supreme authority by proclaiming rights, but by humbling Himself to be perfectly obedient to the Father. He laid aside the privileges of His place in the Godhead and allowed Himself to be the means through which human beings could rediscover their right to be a child of God.

Let this same attitude and purpose and [humble] mind be in you which was in Christ Jesus [Let Him be your example in humility]:

Who although being essentially one with God and in the form of God [possessing the fullness of attributes which make God God], did not think this equality with God was a thing to be eagerly grasped or retained:

But stripped Himself [of all privileges and rightful dignity], *so as to assume the guise of a servant (slave), in that He became like men and was born a human being. And after He appeared in human form He abased and humbled Himself [still further] and carried His obedience to the extreme of death, even the death of the cross! Therefore [because He stooped so low] God has highly exalted Him and has freely bestowed on Him the name that is above every name. Philippians 2:5-9 (AMPC, 1987, bold added)*

Getting right with God

Seeing the oppression in this world today causes most people to yearn for justice. This is a God-given desire and it would be a hopeless situation but for the fact that God is in ultimate authority, is unchanging, and is always ready to hear the prayers of His people, if we humble ourselves.

...and [if] My people who are called by My name humble themselves and pray and seek My face and turn from their wicked ways, then I will hear from heaven, will forgive their sin and will heal their land. 2 Chronicles 7:14

Daniel saw and confessed before God the sinfulness of the people, and turned to Him for justice:

"Lord God, you are great, and we honor you. You are faithful to your covenant ... we have done wrong ... and have turned away from what you showed us was right. We have not listened to your servants the prophets, who spoke in your name to our kings, our rulers, our ancestors, and our whole nation. You, Lord, always do what is right, but we have brought disgrace on ourselves." Daniel 9:4b–7 (GNT)

Jesus, full of grace and truth, is our model today for God's view of true humility and justice, and He offers to be our personal Lord and Saviour. I recently came across a prayer of commitment from the Christian author and pastor A.W. Tozer, which begins by a recognition of how Kingdom living is so very different from the ways of the world:

> *I come to you today, O Lord,*
> *To give up my rights,*
> *To lay down my life,*
> *To offer my future...*

Those following the world can stand on all their supposed rights if they choose, not least on a right of recompense from those who have caused them pain, but followers of Jesus are called to a radical way of obedience and forgiveness.

Finally, here is a prayer to find God's cleansing from any defilement that may have come upon our personal lives through the deception of an ideology, a false religion, which has been far more focussed on the claiming of rights than on the confession of sin:

Heavenly Father, I proclaim that God alone is sovereign and not man. I have let the ways of the world influence me and defile my view of Your Kingdom. Remind me to remain in humble obedience to You and so to avoid the trap of claiming rights that are not from You. I forgive those who have governed the nations of the world and promoted systems of justice that have not been consistent with Your laws.

I have also frequently claimed entitlement <u>from</u> You, whilst not always being obedient <u>to</u> You. Thank You, Lord, that, through my surrender to Jesus, I can be cleansed and restored into knowing the true human rights that You have always intended for Your covenant children, and I can experience all the amazing privileges that flow from that precious relationship.

In Jesus' name, Amen

About the Author

David Cross is Deputy International Director for Ellel Ministries and Regional Director for the Ministry in Western Europe.

He graduated from Nottingham University in 1969 and qualified as a chartered civil engineer, leading to a varied working career, which included building roads and bridges in the Highlands of Scotland and, in the early 1980's, overseeing the construction of new town development in the New Territories area of Hong Kong. It was here that a huge personal change of direction occurred when he gave his life to Jesus.

Returning to Scotland, David became very active in church life and in leading ski tours in the Cairngorm Mountains. In order to further the Christian healing ministry in the Highlands, as an elder in the Church of Scotland, he and others in the local church made contact with Ellel Ministries in 1991, and two years later David and his wife Denise joined the Ministry at the international headquarters of Ellel Grange, near Lancaster.

David and Denise have three children and eight grandchildren, all giving much joy in the midst of very busy lives. Besides the thrill of sharing God's truth through teaching and writing, David loves walking and photography. His authoritative explanation of God's word has brought understanding and healing to many who have been confused and damaged by the ungodly ideologies of today's world. David has written five other books: *Soul-Ties, God's Covering, Trapped by Control, The Dangers of Alternative Ways of Healing* (with John Berry) and the *A-Z Guide to the Healing Ministry.*

Other Books by David Cross

www.sovereignworld.com

Soul Ties, The Unseen Bond in Relationships
David Cross
Providing unique insight, this book looks discerningly at what a soul tie is, both of a good and bad kind, and the impact this invisible bond has on us in our everyday life.
Paperback 128 pages
ISBN 978–185240–451–2

The Dangers of Alternative Ways to Healing, How to Avoid New Age Deceptions
David Cross and John Berry
Many forms of alternative therapies are available today and this book provides fascinating coverage of what they are with clear guidelines on how spiritually safe or unsafe they might be.
Paperback 176 pages
ISBN 978–185240–537–3

Trapped by Control, How to Find Freedom
David Cross
This book takes a closer look at who or what can control people's lives and how to escape from ungodly control by others.
Paperback 112 pages
ISBN 978–185240–501–4

God's Covering – A Place of Healing
David Cross
Seeks to explain the reality of what can happen when we move out from under God's covering and become spiritually exposed.
Paperback 192 pages
ISBN 978–185240–485–7

A-Z Guide to the Healing Ministry
David Cross
In David Cross's A – Z Guide to the Healing Ministry of Jesus you will find answers to almost every question you could ever have about the healing and deliverance ministries. This is much more than a reference book for occasional use – Peter Horrobin describes it as "a healing goldmine"! This is a compendium of truth that will bring you to the person and presence of Jesus.
Hardback 480 pages
ISBN 978–1–85240–755–1

All these books and more are available from Sovereign World.

Sovereign World Ltd

Please visit our online shop to browse our range of titles.
www.sovereignworld.com
or write to the company at the headquarters address:

Sovereign World Ltd.
Ellel Grange
Bay Horse
Lancaster
Lancashire LA2 0HN
United Kingdom

Or email us at:
info@sovereignworld.com

*Most books are also available in e-book format
and can be purchased online.*

Would You Join With Us To Bless the Nations?

At the Sovereign World Trust, our mandate and passion is to send books, like the one you've just read, to *faithful leaders who can equip others* (2 Tim 2:2).

The 'Good News' is that in all of the poorest nations we reach, the Kingdom of God is growing in an accelerated way but, to further this Great Commission work, the Pastors and Leaders in these countries need good teaching resources in order to provide sound Biblical doctrine to their flock, their future generations and especially new converts.

If you could donate a copy of this or other titles from Sovereign World Ltd, you will be helping to supply much-needed resources to Pastors and Leaders in many countries.

Contact us for more information on (+44)(0)1732 851150 or visit our website www.sovereignworldtrust.org.uk

> *"I have all it takes to further my studies. Sovereign is making it all possible for me"*
>
> **Rev. Akfred Keyas – Kenya**

> *"My ministry is rising up gradually since I have been teaching people from these books"*
>
> **Pastor John Obaseki – Nigeria**